Suzanne Shepherd and Anna Levine in a scene from the Yale Repertory Theatre production of "Johnny Bull."

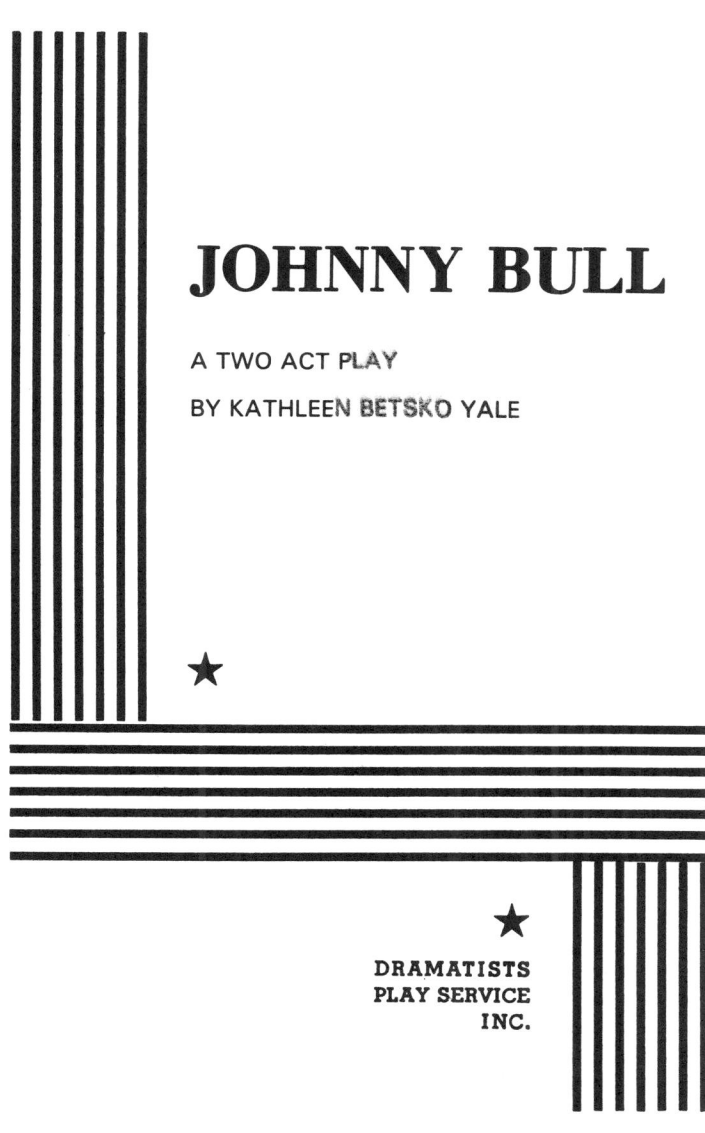

JOHNNY BULL

A TWO ACT PLAY

BY KATHLEEN BETSKO YALE

★

★

DRAMATISTS
PLAY SERVICE
INC.

SOUND EFFECTS

An audio cassette containing the sound effects which may be used in connection with production of this play, can be obtained from Thomas J. Valentino, Inc., 151 West 46th Street, New York, N.Y. 10036.

Baseball crowd
Baby crying
Dogs barking, angry dogs
Rifle shots
Auto sounds

SPECIAL NOTE ON SONGS AND RECORDINGS

For performance of such songs and recordings mentioned in this play as are in copyright, the permission of the copyright owners must be obtained; or other songs and recordings in the public domain substituted.

For Candy, Stephen and Aaron Marcus

With respect and appreciation for the mining families of
America's coal towns

JOHNNY BULL received its world premiere production at the Yale Repertory Theatre (Lloyd Richards, Artistic Director) in New Haven, Connecticut, on April 9, 1982. It was directed by Mr. Richards; the settings were by Joel Fontaine; the costumes were by Gene K. Lakin; and the lighting was by Stephen Strawbridge. The cast was as follows:

IRIS .... Anna Levine
MARIE (The Mother) .... Suzanne Shepherd
KATRINE (The Sister) .... Rikke Borge
STEPHAN (The Father) .... Jamie Schmitt
JOE .... Kevin Geer

The play is set in Willard Patch, a tiny coal mining hamlet in the Monongahela Valley in Pennsylvania. The time is early autumn, 1959, a period of severe economic recession in this region of the United States.

JOHNNY BULL was originally presented as a staged reading at the Eugene O'Neill Theater Center's 1981 National Playwrights Conference.

CHARACTERS

IRIS KOVACS — 18 years old. A working-class English girl.

JOE KOVACS — About 21. Iris's American husband. Recently discharged from the United States Air Force.

MARIE KOVACS — Early 50's. Joe's Hungarian-born mother.

STEPHAN KOVACS — Late 50's. Joe's Hungarian-born father. A coal miner.

KATRINE KOVACS — Early 30's. Joe's retarded sister.

JOHNNY BULL

The stage is in total darkness. A spotlight comes up, Stage Left, on a young, English girl with a Midlands working-class accent. She is wearing a cheap raincoat and head scarf. She stands outside of the set and addresses the audience in an animated, matter-of-fact sort of way.

IRIS. Funny how some people get married and hardly know each other, isn't it? I mean, it's all chance. What would have happened if you hadn't got off the bus at the wrong stop or walked by accident down a particular street? You might never have ended up with who you ended up with, might you? I know one thing: if I'd stayed in my little room behind the fish 'n' chip shop and done me ironing—instead of going to that dance at the American air base—I'd never have met Joe Kovacs. It was all Freda Wilkinson's fault. Freda was my best friend back then. She was nice—a bit bossy, you know—but nice. Anyway, she was late, as usual. And there I was, all by meself in the ladies loo at the N.C.O club. I don't mind admitting I was a bit depressed because of my appearance. Have you ever felt like that? Me hair was supposed to have been in one of those "beehive" things that were all the rage back then . . . teased up to here. Remember? Beehive! It looked more like a lopsided bird's nest stuck on top of me head. No joking. If I'd stepped outside with that blinkin' hairdo, some low-flying pigeon would have laid eggs in it. And, to add insult to devastation, I was wearing this dress I'd made meself. I'd seen one like it in a Doris Day picture and tried to copy it. Talk about Christian-bloody-Dior run amok! Here I thought I was going to be a symphony in red velvet. Should've seen me. Bloody Hell! I looked more like I'd been caught in an air raid—all coming apart at the seams. Well, I never was much with a needle . . . not your domestic type at all, really. (*Titters.*) But anyway, there I stood wondering whether to set fire to meself or go home when in bounces old Freda. (*Very animated.*) She shouts: "C'mon . . . c'mon . . . you daft twit! I've got this Yank I want you to meet!" And I said: "Nooo, no. No, I don't feel like it!" And she said:

7

"You will when you see him, he's a smasher, this one." "Ooohh," I says back, "like that Tech Sergeant with the pimples you stuck me with last week?" "*No!*", she carries on, "*this* one's from California, I think!" Well, *that* did it. *California!* That's where all the film stars live, you know. I remember thinking there was a remote possibility this chap might live next door to one . . . so Freda takes a punch or two at the old bird's nest, sticks a pin in me dress — and with a dab of "Ashes of Roses" behind each ear, I raced off for an exotic encounter. Well, as you might have guessed, he wasn't from California. (*Beat.*) Pennsylvania. Willard Patch, Pennsylvania. (*Sighs.*) Ever so nice, though . . . laughed at everything I said. The accent, you know. It tickled him. Anyway, we took a bit of a fancy to each other . . . and became very close. (*Beat.*) Soooooo close, as a matter of fact, I ended up with a bun in the oven. Well, we were only teenagers. I don't remember either of us thinking very much about it. We just went out and got married. (*She exits. The spotlight fades. In the black, an accordian begins playing a Hungarian folk tune.*)

ACT I

SCENE 1

The lights come up on a simple, spotless kitchen, located in Willard Patch — a tiny coal mining village in Appalachia. There are several doors: one to a closet where outdoor clothing and guns are kept; one to a living room; one to the outside with screen; and one at the top of a small flight of stairs, with curtains across, leading to an upstairs hallway that provides access to the bedrooms. One bedroom is seen up and off to one side; it has a door to the rear wall that leads into this hallway. The kitchen is furnished with a hutch; a large wooden table on which stand enamel pans containing rising bread dough covered with damp towels; several straight-back chairs; and, most prominent, an enormous coal stove. In one corner is a primitive wooden sink with an iron pump. The walls are hung with religious pictures and ancient family photographs. On top of the stove are two large, galvanized tubs of hot water, a pan of steaming Hungarian food, and a pot of coffee. Somewhere on the set: an old but beautiful accordian. As the play begins, we see Marie, a

8

heavy Hungarian-born woman in her early fifties, spreading newspapers over the floor. Assisting her is her slightly retarded daughter, Katrine, about thirty years old. She has the mind of a twelve-year-old, a stubborn, cunning nature and a sullen manner of speaking. There are no physical manifestations of her handicap. Both women wear faded housedresses, thick stockings and babushkas.

The time is early evening in the fall of 1959. It is growing dark outside. There is a kerosene lamp on the table, and, on the wall, very much out of place, is a brand-new bright red telephone.

MARIE. (*Hungarian accent.*) When Daddy come in, you be nice. (*She lights the lamp.*) You don't make him mad with talk about Joe's new wife.

KATRINE. I wish her ship would sink.

MARIE. Son of God forgive her for the way she was born. Help me lift the tub! I said: Help me lift! Ready? (*The two women lift the heavy tub off the stove and balance it on two chairs.*) Oi-yoi-yoi. Now look what you did. I should have left you up on the mountain when you were born and let the damn bears eat you.

KATRINE. Why Joe have to go get that Johnny Bull wife? Can't she get here by herself? Is she so dumb?

MARIE. You will be dumb, big cow . . . if I hear you say Johnny Bull again.

KATRINE. Daddy say it.

MARIE. I don't care what your father say . . . (*She sets another chair by the tub with a pan of rinse water.*) . . . you don't say. Johnny Bull is insult. You say English. Joe's wife is from England. Give me clean towels! Hurry! Her name is Iris . . . I.I.ris. An' you better watch your mouth to her, I'm warning you.

KATRINE. (*Sullen.*) She's gonna have a kid, ain't she?

MARIE. Everybody is allowed one mistake. (*She pulls small screen from closet and hangs clean clothing over it.*)

KATRINE. She's a whore!

MARIE. That's all I can take. Now you gonna get what you been asking for! (*Grabs broom and swipes at Katrine.*)

KATRINE. That's what Daddy say!

MARIE. That . . . ain't . . .

KATRINE. O . . . O . . . Ow.

9

MARIE. . . . Your . . . businesses . . .

KATRINE. Oo . . . Oww!

MARIE. You Hungarian ox! (*Sound of a car.*)

KATRINE. It's Joe. (*She runs to the window.*)

MARIE. It's Daddy. Pour that coffee. You don't say *nothin'* about Joe, 'less you want the good Lord to strike you dead. And if *He* don't . . . *I* will!

KATRINE. I rather *be* dead than livin' with Johnny Bulls.

MARIE. We wash Daddy . . . feed him . . . give him his vodka. Maybe I get him upstairs and asleep before Joe gets home . . . (*They put on large aprons.*) And when you are finished with your work, you get outa this kitchen and into your room. (*Sounds of dogs barking, heavy boots dropping.*)

KATRINE. You give my brother my room. Now I ain't got no room.

MARIE. (*Women's voices drop to urgent whispers.*) You got Joe's old room.

KATRINE. I want *my* room!

MARIE. You lucky I don't tie you up on a leash outside . . . (*The door crashes open; Stephan, a big man, about sixty years old but still proud and rugged, stands framed in the doorway. He is a coal miner, and except for his boots which he has left on the porch, is exactly as he left the mine, covered in coal dust and still wearing his helmet.*) Put pig's feet in stove, Katrine!

STEPHAN. (*Slight Hungarian accent.*) She givin' you trouble?

MARIE. No. (*She takes his helmet, wipes it, and hangs it up.*)

STEPHAN. I whip her damn ass she don't listen!

MARIE. Hush up, old man . . . stay on the newspaper. You think I got nothin' better to do than clean up your coal dust from my house?

STEPHAN. From next week there will be no more coal dust . . . (*He takes off shirt and drops it in pail of water that Katrine brings.*) Where's Joe?

KATRINE. He went . . .

MARIE. (*Slaps Katrine.*) Wash that dinner bucket!

KATRINE. Only got one pair hands. (*Stephan bends over and washes face.*)

MARIE. So it's final, Daddy? From next week you laid off?

STEPHAN. You know it was coming, Marie.

MARIE. Why the union don't do somethin'?

STEPHAN. Because they just as big crooks now as the goddamn bosses.

MARIE. It ain't the union . . . not the one we fought for. We put good people in. What the hell happened?

STEPHAN. Katrine! Bring me Vodka!

MARIE. Oi-yoi . . . what we gonna do, Stephan? (*Katrine brings vodka, then the two women begin to wash the upper half of Stephan's body.*)

STEPHAN. Did you starve yet? All right! Take care women's business and let me take care mine. And don't pretend to me, Marie. Don't protect Joe like a baby from me. I know he went to New York last night.

MARIE. Is it news? He went to get his wife from ship.

KATRINE. She's a Johnny Bull. (*Marie shakes her fist at Katrine.*)

STEPHAN. That Buick ain't gonna make it back here. Goddamn piece a' junk.

MARIE. Who's fault is that?

STEPHAN. I told him I don't want no Johnny Bull English in my house.

MARIE. For shame you big Hunkie foreigner.

STEPHAN. They come over here . . . take the best damn jobs in our mines . . .

MARIE. Soap, Kattie.

STEPHAN. Get top jobs in the union, and why?

MARIE. Because from England they speak English. Big surprise. Hold out your arms.

STEPHAN. English . . . everywhere they go they take over . . . make trouble . . . (*Pause.*) Why you think we fight in this country? To get rid of kings! To get a president.

MARIE. You show your son respect. He's a man now.

STEPHAN. He's a whoremaster.

MARIE. Hush. Pitchers got big ears. Go feed the dogs, girl! Move. (*Katrine ignores her.*) Out! Before I put you to bed!

MARIE AND STEPHEN. (*In unison.*) Out!

KATRINE. I ain't got no bed. (*She exits outside.*)

STEPHAN. He coulda had all the whores he wanted. He didn't have to bring them here. Same goddamn thing as his brother.

MARIE. (*Sarcastic.*) I thought you only had *one* son. (*Pouring him another vodka.*)

STEPHAN. One son is all I got left. And I wait three years for *that* sumbitch to come home.

MARIE. (*Pouring rinse water over him.*) Drink your vodka!

STEPHAN. And now he's back under my roof. And what I say means nothing?

MARIE. Oi-yoi-yoi, Istvan.

STEPHAN. Who raised him? Hah?

MARIE. You did.

STEPHAN. Who fed him?

MARIE. Nobody went without, Daddy.

STEPHAN. Joe has a responsibility to this house . . . as in the Old Country . . . and to you, his mother.

MARIE. This ain't Old Country.

STEPHAN. And a responsibility to me, his father . . . and to his sister out there. Who will take care of her when we drop dead I want to know?

KATRINE. (*Rushing in.*) They here, Mama. The car is here. *He's got her!* Joe's got the Johnny Bull!

MARIE. My God! (*She hurriedly takes off apron, spits on it, wipes Katrine's face.*) All right! Go finish washing your father!

STEPHAN. You gonna leave me naked? (*Marie puts a screen around him; his head and shoulders are still visible.*) Goddamn it!

MARIE. (*Urgent.*) Be nice, Daddy.

STEPHAN. I don't want no whore in my house!

MARIE. God forgive you, oi-yoi-yoi . . . (*The door opens. Joe comes in with suitcases. After a couple of seconds Iris enters, noticeably apprehensive. She is wearing vivid lipstick, a gaudy coat, high heels, long sequined earrings, and carrying a gold plastic handbag: She looks like a Woolworth's Christmas tree ornament. The family can hardly be blamed for thinking she might be a whore.*)

JOE. Hi, everybody! Iris . . . this is my folks.

IRIS. (*Very uncomfortable, very English.*) Hello! (*Pause.*) Well, I'm . . . ah . . . very pleased to meet you I'm sure.

JOE. Dad, this is my wife, Iris. (*Pause. Stephan disappears behind screen washing loudly.*) Mamma?

MARIE. (*Expressionless.*) That's nice you come, ain't it, Daddy? (*Pause.*) Katrine, you say hello to your brother's wife. You say nice, now! (*To Iris.*) She can't help it. (*Marie grabs Katrine's arm.*) I warned you . . .

KATRINE. I gotta slop this coal water.

JOE. Say hello to my wife.

IRIS. It's all right, Joe.

JOE. It ain't all right.

IRIS. I think she's just shy . . . aren't you?

JOE. You say hi!

KATRINE. No.

IRIS. (*To Joe.*) *I* used to be rude when I was shy. It's all right.

JOE. I said: say hi!

KATRINE. She got my room! It's *my* room! Why don't you stay where you come from, Johnny Bull whore!

JOE. Sonofabitch! (*He tries to smack Katrine.*)

STEPHAN. Jesus Christ!

JOE. I'll kill her, Momma . . . I swear . . .

IRIS. No, Joe!

MARIE. Leave her! Leave her, Joe! You know she can't help it! Stop! You're gonna hurt somebody! Jesus . . . Mary, Mother of God! (*Katrine screams, Joe curses, the dogs outside are barking and somewhere there is the distant sound of an accordian playing Hungarian music. Iris speaks to the audience. Whenever she does this, the family go about their business, as unobtrusively as possible and seem completely unaware of her. She removes her coat, revealing a short skirt and skimpy blouse to which she has sewn, rather tastelessly, a few multicolored sequins. Marie ladles food onto plates at the stove. Stephan is still behind the screen. Katrine, sulking, begins to dry his back.*)

IRIS. Well, that lot came as quite a shock I can tell you. I thought I was going to Hollywood. Honest to God, I thought I was going right straight into the middle of a bloody Doris Day movie. (*She sits at the table and is back in the scene.*)

JOE. (*To Katrine.*) An' I better not hear another damn word outa you! Show Iris the phone I got her, Momma! You see the phone I got you, Iris? (*He exits to the bedroom with suitcase.*) And don't go given' her none a' that garlic! She ain't never had none a' that garlic shit!

MARIE. (*Sternly. Iris is just another mouth to feed.*) Garlic good for you.

IRIS. Ah . . . no, thank you . . . really . . .

JOE'S VOICE. (*From bedroom.*) We got no night bucket.

MARIE. (*To Joe.*) In the attic! (*To Iris.*) L'il bit pigs feet, maybe.

IRIS. What kind of feet?

STEPHAN'S VOICE. (*From behind the screen.*) Pig's feet! Ain't she never had no pig's feet, for Chrissakes?

MARIE. Pig's feet nice! You try now! (*She places foot in front of Iris. Upstairs Joe disappears from bedroom.*)

IRIS. (*Nauseated at the smell of unfamiliar food.*) Well . . . umhh . . . see, I . . .

MARIE. I don't like good food to go to waste.

IRIS. Well, perhaps . . . a bit later . . . (*Trying to change the subject.*) Oohh, it's a lovely telephone, Mrs. Kovacs. I've only ever seen one on the street, never inside a house before.

MARIE. That's the kinda son I got . . . had that put in special for you.

IRIS. Thank you ever so much.

MARIE. Don't thank me. Thank the Lord God you got good husband. (*She exits upstairs with suitcase.*)

KATRINE. (*To Stephan.*) We ain't never needed no phone before!

IRIS. (*To audience.*) See, I'd been mad to come to America ever since I was little. Long before I ever saw Doris-bloody-Day prancing across the silver screen. I think it all started with this American magazine I found once. I don't think I could even read. I just remember the colors . . . all bright colors . . . the houses, the clothes . . . colored and shiny. Even the food was shiny. And people had lovely brown skin from all the sun. I could just imagine meself lying under a palm tree all day, getting brown as a berry, not a care in the world. Know what I mean?

KATRINE. She ain't eatin'.

STEPHAN. What's wrong with my food? (*He emerges from behind the screen, buttoning a clean shirt.*)

IRIS. Oh, *nothing* . . . nothing at all . . .

STEPHAN. We send food packages to keep Johnny Bulls alive in the war and now you turn up your nose at my table?

IRIS. Oh, no. It's just I've never had . . . (*Beat.*) *feet* . . . before. Ahm, I suppose . . . they'll grow on me . . . after a while. P'raps a cup of tea would be . . .

KATRINE. We don't drink no tea.

STEPHAN. Give her coffee! (*He takes hunting rifle from closet, Katrine pours coffee. Stephan keeps his distance and never looks at Iris*

14

directly — not while she's looking at him, anyway — throughout the entire scene.)

IRIS. I wonder . . . have you got a drop of milk?

KATRINE. No.

STEPHAN. Get her the milk! (*He begins to clean his gun.*)

IRIS. (*Pleasantly.*) Ahmm . . . is California close to here? (*Pause.*) Lovely name, isn't it . . . California? Exotic. (*Pause.*) I once saw a picture of it . . . in a magazine . . . and there was a tree with lemons growing on it. Even now, I can't hardly imagine lemons growing on trees. I don't know where I thought they came from . . . but *not* trees. (*Pause.*) Have *you* got any lemon trees? In the garden, I mean?

STEPHAN. I wait three years for that boy to come home here . . . help paint this house.

IRIS. Absence does make the heart grow fonder, doesn't it?

STEPHAN. You know how many times he wrote his Momma? The one who wipe his ass how many years?

IRIS. I . . . ahh . . .

STEPHAN. Never!

IRIS. Oh, I gave him a piece of my mind about that, all right . . . (*The gun seems pointed in her direction. Iris politely moves her chair out of the line of fire.*) In a *nice* way, I mean; I said: You're lucky to have a Mum and Dad. You ought to write, I said.

STEPHAN. That boy is all I got. (*Indicates Katrine.*) You think I get comfort from this one? Six weeks he's back in this country. He got soft in England. When he was a baby I taught him how to hold a gun . . . when he was no higher than this. (*Crosses to the door with gun.*)

MARIE. (*Entering.*) Put that gun down, Old Fool, and come eat! Kattie! Take down the screen.

KATRINE. How come *she* don't do no work?

MARIE. You want me to put you to bed?

KATRINE. *She* got my bed!

IRIS. (*To audience.*) I bet you're wondering why I didn't turn round, right there and then, and go back to England. P'raps I would've if I'd had the money . . . if I'd known better. Still, it wasn't all roses in England either. I'm from what you might call an industrial section . . . slums if you want to know the truth. If I was to be really honest, I'd have to say I didn't have much to

15

go back to . . . I mean, no Mum or Dad or anything. (*While Iris is talking, Katrine and Marie accomplish the nightly chores moving in perfect time with each other — a natural coordination that comes from years of performing the same rituals. Newspaper from the floor is twisted into fire kindling, chairs replaced against the wall, and finally each takes a handle of the wash tubs and hauls them outside.*) See, (*Quite cheerfully.*) I got evacuated when I was a baby in the war . . . from the bombs, you know . . . and I never got back home. Nobody came to fetch me when it was over. Wasn't just me. Happened to hundreds of kids. That's war for you. Shove you on a train with a number round your neck. What can you do? When you separate people like that, by the thousands, you're bound to lose some of them, aren't you? (*Stephan watches after the women from the screen door with his gun as they go in and out with pitchers and pans to be hung on the porch.*) Anyway, as you can imagine, I was rather looking forward to having a real Mum and Dad, Joe's Mum and Dad . . . and here I'd been thinking *they* were looking forward to having *me*.

STEPHAN. (*Calling out to women.*) I'm watchin' younse, don't worry! (*To Iris.*) We gotta watch out for our women aroun' here.

IRIS. Oh . . .

STEPHAN. Gotta lotta white trash . . . gotta lotta niggers over them tracks out there. (*He yells outside again.*) Marie, I got my eye on you!

MARIE. (*Entering.*) I don't need no watchin', Old Man.

STEPHAN. Kattie! Get in here!

MARIE. (*Sternly to Iris.*) Eat! Skinny woman no good! No good for makin' babies. (*She exits again.*)

STEPHAN. (*Alone with Iris, he examines her for a second. He speaks with an odd combination of gruff shyness and irritation.*) You know how much England owes this country?

IRIS. No.

STEPHAN. Take a guess.

IRIS. How much?

STEPHAN. (*His irritation mounts gradually.*) Plenty! That's why we ain't got no jobs because half the world owes us money and we're too soft to try to collect. Men work all their lives here. For what? To end up on welfare?

JOE. (*Entering.*) Hey, nobody's gonna end up on the welfare,

Daddy. You don't have to eat that stuff, Iris. (*Shouts out the door.*) Kattie, make Iris a sandwich!

STEPHAN. Before welfare come in this house I would kill everyone here.

MARIE. (*Entering with Katrine.*) So kill, Old Fool. It will be good for the neighborhood.

JOE. Oh, that's *real* nice in front a' my wife.

STEPHAN. This is a free country.

MARIE. Who's free?

JOE. (*Fiercely to Katrine.*) I said: Make Iris a sandwich!

KATRINE. She ain't *my* wife.

MARIE. (*To Stephan.*) Did Eisenhower ever help *you*? You know who paid the strikebreakers?

JOE. (*To Katrine.*) You insult my wife again, girl, you'll be a sorrier sight on two fat legs than you are now. (*He cuffs her.*)

STEPHAN. (*To Marie.*) She thinks that king is such a big shot.

MARIE. Your damn president . . . *that's* who paid 'em. (*Stephan suddenly fires his gun out the door. Everyone dashes outside except Iris who remains at the table, eyes wide with horror.*)

STEPHAN'S VOICE. There he goes! That sumabitch runnin' across my squash patch again! (*He fires again.*) I'll get your black ass one a these day, Wiggins! (*Stephan re-enters. After a moment, he speaks pointedly to Iris.*) Nobody comes through here that don't belong . . . (*Beat.*) Not without trouble. (*Iris realizes that the gauntlet has been thrown. Overcoming her distaste for the strange food, she slowly, deliberately, picks up the pig's foot and takes a bite.*)

IRIS. You're wrong, Mr. Kovacs.

STEPHAN. Hmmm?

IRIS. It's not a king, you know.

STEPHAN. What?

IRIS. I said: England hasn't got a king. Haven't had one for years. He died. We've got a queen now. (*The lights fade gradually. Stephan, still holding his gun, strides upstairs. A spotlight remains on Iris. She puts the pig's foot down, speaks to audience.*) Now. . . . I'd never *seen* a gun before, let alone heard one fired. Guns. Guns. Guns. Joe's Dad carried his everywhere. Always taking potshots at nextdoor's cat. . . . not to mention poor Mr. Wiggins. He took that rifle out to the loo, up to the bar . . . (*Points upstairs.*) Even took it to bed with him . . . right up the stairs, like a baby, every single night. (*She gathers her belongings and heads towards the*

17

bedroom.) Bloody hell. I thought I'd ended up in a John Wayne picture. (*She exits. The spotlight fades to black. A plaintive Hungarian melody on the accordian rises in the darkness and continues until the next scene.*)

ACT I

SCENE 2

The next morning. Bedroom.
This room contains heavy, old furniture: a large high bed with goosefeather ticks and an ancient chest of drawers. Next to the bed is a large enamel bucket with a lid. Iris, wearing only a slip, is applying makeup in a hand mirror, by the window. Marie enters with a suitcase followed by Katrine.

IRIS. Oh . . . morning, Mrs. Kovacs. (*Uncomfortable pause.*) I was just thinking I'd like to run out there and shovel that big coal mine away . . . see what's behind it.
MARIE. (*Pulls down the blind. Her attitude here is one of stern practicality. If there's to be peace in the Kovacs' house, she must teach this girl how to fit in — and quickly.*) What's behind it is the same as what's in front of it, believe me. (*She puts suitcase on bed.*) The drawers are clean. You unpack this bag, OK? A place for everything and everything in its place. (*She picks up Iris's lace panties from the floor with disapproval.*)
IRIS. Oh, sorry. (*Rushes to pick up her bra.*) I was just about to do that.
MARIE. We don't want no more work that there already is. (*She exits.*)
IRIS. No . . . (*She goes to dresser mirror and applies perfume.*)
KATRINE. (*A sullen challenge.*) What's that stuff younse puttin'?
IRIS. Scent . . . "Ashes of Roses." Want a dab?
KATRINE. Stinks worst than a skunk fart.
IRIS. There's no need to be rude.
KATRINE. Where younse goin'?
IRIS. (*Applying rouge enthusiastically.*) Oh, I thought I'd have a quick look round the shops.

KATRINE. (*Hollering out the door.*) Momma . . . she's gettin' set to go out! (*To Iris.*) There ain't no stores.

IRIS. There must be something.

KATRINE. Jus' Mikey's General.

IRIS. Well, I'll go there, then. Do you want to come with me?

KATRINE. I ain't 'llowed.

IRIS. Why ever not?

KATRINE. (*Steps outside door yells to her mother again.*) She's puttin' lipstick, Momma!

IRIS. Excuse me, I *am* a grown up, you know! (*To audience.*) Cheek! She watched every move I made. I don't like being watched. Never have done. Still, I knew it was no good getting me knickers in a twist over that one. More important was to find out where I was. I hadn't the foggiest idea! I mean, I knew I was in Pennsylvania . . . but where the Hell was Pennsylvania? (*To Katrine as she reenters.*) I don't suppose you'd happen to have a map, would you? One that shows California.

KATRINE. Daddy got one.

IRIS. Oh, good.

KATRINE. He ain't gonna show it to ya.

MARIE. (*Entering with dust mop.*) Finish your work, Girl.

IRIS. (*Firmly, as she puts on sequin-dotted blouse.*) Mrs. Kovacs . . . I'm just popping out for a bit . . . (*Defiantly in Katrine's direction.*) *If* nobody minds.

MARIE. Out?

IRIS. Oh, just to have a quick look round.

MARIE. Today is Tuesday.

KATRINE. Wash day.

MARIE. Here to wash clothes takes all day. *We* get up at five. *We* fetch water . . .

KATRINE. (*Assisting Marie.*) Heat tubs on the stove.

MARIE. (*Folding back the ticks to the rhythm of the words.*) And then we wash, we boil, we rinse. Hang them out. Then wash and boil and rinse and hang out some more.

IRIS. Sounds like a lot of clothes.

MARIE. There's plenty coal dust here and big men to keep clean. (*She points out the window.*) I put already three lines wash out while you were sleepin'.

IRIS. So . . . I shan't be going out today, I take it? (*Pause.*) Perhaps tomorrow, then.

19

MARIE. Wednesday we iron.

IRIS. All day?

KATRINE. All day.

MARIE. Go stir the soup, girl. *Move!* (*Katrine exits. Marie gets down under the bed with the mop. Only her rear end and legs are visible.*)

IRIS. Oh well . . . perhaps the weekend? (*To the audience, removing fancy blouse.*) Blimey . . . I had more freedom in reform school than I had in Willard Patch. Mind you, I'd not much intention of ironing meself into an early grave. Freda used to say: The world is full of willing workers. Some willing to work . . . and some willing to let them. You can imagine which category I fell under.

MARIE. (*Emerges from beneath the bed.*) How old are you?

IRIS. Eighteen.

MARIE. I was already old woman by eighteen.

IRIS. In England we say you're only as old as you feel.

MARIE. That case, I shoulda been dead long time ago. (*She shakes pillows.*)

JOE. (*Entering.*) Hey, look at my two girls together. (*Kisses mother.*) Ain't she sump'n, Momma? She makin' you laugh? I told her she couldn't come here less she made you laugh . . .

MARIE. In the morning, we wipe the dust mop good into the corners and take the rugs downstairs to shake. (*Joe laughs and shakes his finger at Iris.*) Today, *I* do them. Tomorrow, *you* begin work. (*MARIE puts the rugs over her arm.*) Women have to be strong here. (*Joe flexes his muscles.*) Nobody ain't gonna baby you.

IRIS. Nobody ever has.

MARIE. Good . . . (*She picks up sequin blouse and goes to door.*) Then you won't miss it. (*She exits.*)

JOE. I tell you what *I* missed. I missed you. Six weeks! I near went crazy waitin' for you. (*He swings Iris around.*) Hey, what's a' matter? You don't like it here, do you?

IRIS. I didn't exactly get a warm welcome, did I?

JOE. I knew you didn't like it.

IRIS. I've only spent one night, Duckie. Give me a chance. (*She wanders to window and puts up the blind.*) How long are we going to live here, Joe?

JOE. I don't know. Till I get a job, I guess . . . get me some lumber . . . build us a l'il house down the end of the yard.

IRIS. (*Slow turn to look at him.*) This yard?

JOE. Yep. Why?

IRIS. I just wondered. (*Pause.*) How come everyone goes deaf here when you mention California?

JOE. My brother, Pishta*, lit out for the West coast few years back. He was the big shot for Daddy. Don't ask me why . . . asshole never did nothin' for the old man but break his heart. Anyway, Pishta's on the "Dead and Deserted" list now.

IRIS. What a shame!

JOE. Daddy'll be OK . . . He's got me now.

IRIS. How far is California?

JOE. 'Bout three thousand miles.

IRIS. Three *thousand?* I don't believe you. That's how far it is to England!

JOE. (*He lays back on bed, pulling a pillow over his face.*) That's right, Babycakes.

IRIS. (*To audience.*) Well, that's the bloody trouble with the English. They have no idea how vast America is. They think they can nip over to the Grand Canyon, run across to New York, pop to Florida and be back in time for tea. Well, I soon found out it wasn't a matter of nipping and popping. Where Joe lived, it took half a day to get to Woolworth's and back!

JOE. (*Sitting up suddenly.*) Hey! Did it bother you to use the bucket?

IRIS. Not really. Where do I empty it?

JOE. Kattie does that.

IRIS. I'll do me own dirty work, thank you.

JOE. You're gonna have to do things the way *we* do 'em. She ain't right in the head. That's her job. Momma likes to keep her busy. It's good for her. (*Joining Iris at the window.*) See that l'il buildin'? Way over? Where that mangy ol' shepherd dog is?

IRIS. Yes.

JOE. That's where she takes it. That's the outhouse. (*Proudly.*) That there, woman, is a luxury item! That there is a *two*-holer.

*Pronounced: "PEE-SHTA"

21

I helped my ol' man build that when I was a kid. 'Fore that we only had a oner.

IRIS. Does that mean we can go together?

JOE. Unh-huh.

IRIS. Well, at least we've got somewhere we can be by ourselves.

JOE. And over yonder . . . there's where ol' man Wiggins lives . . . in that rickety shack. Him and Daddy been feudin' for years. Some people don't talk too nice about colored here, Iris. We don't mix . . . (*He moves away.*) and you can't neither.

IRIS. I will if I want to.

JOE. You'll do as you're told.

IRIS. Oh, will I?

JOE. (*Sharply.*) Look; kid . . . you're in America . . . it's different here.

IRIS. I think you're different, too. You're not the same as you were in England.

JOE. I'm the same. I'm a little edgy is all. Ever'body's edgy. You'll be OK. We'll check out a good doctor tomorrow and . . . (*As he pats her tummy, Katrine enters.*) You're supposed to knock before you go in somebody's room.

KATRINE. I don't have to *knock* on my *own* door!

JOE. It's my door now! Just take that bucket and git! Go see Momma . . . Go on!

KATRINE. No!

JOE. (*Threatening.*) Kattie, get your ass outa here . . . now! (*She still defies him.*) I told you . . . I warned you . . . (*There's a scuffle. Katrine dives for the door.*)

IRIS. Joe . . . Joe . . . don't (*Joe runs after Katrine.*)

KATRINE'S VOICE. (*Running downstairs.*) Daddy gonna fix you, boy! He don't want that Johnny Bull whore here. He gonna gimme my room back, you'll see! (*Sounds of slap and a scream.*)

JOE'S VOICE. And next time you run your mouth, it's gonna be worse . . . (*He reenters.*)

IRIS. Why do you keep hitting her?

JOE. She asked for it! (*Beat.*) She'll stand there till she makes you do it. Ask Momma. A slap is the same as a goddamn kiss to her.

IRIS. She can't help it!

JOE. You don't know nothin' about what goes on here. So don't stick your nose where it don't belong. (*A hurt silence ensues. Joe softens.*) Hey . . . get dressed and come on downstairs. I'll show you my high school yearbook. You can see how fat I was.

IRIS. You weren't, were you?

JOE. Like a pig. Still think I'm handsome?

IRIS. Just like Elvis. (*They laugh. He spins her into a jitterbug singing "Blue Suede Shoes."* She twirls to the window, he "scissor-splits" in the other direction.*) Joe, what's all this wire over the windows for?

JOE. Screens . . . keeps the tarantulas out.

IRIS. Tarantulas? (*Really frightened.*) Not the ones with the big hairy legs?

JOE. Just like your'n. (*He advances on her playfully. She screams.*)

IRIS. No . . . oo . . . *is there?*

JOE. An' you better check your shoes every mornin'.

IRIS. Why?

JOE. That's where they like to go to bed. (*He jumps at her.*) An' they bite like this! On the neck . . . on the titty . . .

IRIS. (*Pushing him away.*) Oh, you are a liar . . . (*Pulling her dress on.*) There's no tarantulas in Pennsylvania.

JOE. How do you know?

IRIS. My God!

JOE. What?

IRIS. Somebody's let my dress down.

JOE. You're crazy!

IRIS. It's down to me ankles.

JOE. It ain't ruined, is it?

IRIS. That's not the point!

JOE. It's probably my mother.

IRIS. She went in my suitcases.

JOE. She just wants to make it easier for you with my Dad.

IRIS. (*After a pause.*) Because he thinks I'm a whore? You might as well say it, Joe.

JOE. He's been the way he is for sixty years. I can't change him.

*See Special Note on copyright page.

23

IRIS. What have I done wrong?

JOE. You got pregnant before you were married.

IRIS. And that makes me a whore?

JOE. I didn't say that.

IRIS. I wouldn't have come here if I'd known.

JOE. Look, any woman got the nerve to move *into* this Patch is a whore . . . and anybody got the guts to *leave* is no damn good. That's the way he sees it. It ain't *you*. It's him. C'mon, Kid . . . soon's he sees what a good wife you're gonna be, he'll come around.

IRIS. How long will that take?

JOE. Ohhh . . . I figure that first twenty years is gonna be the worst. Now I don't wanna see anymore a that hang-doggin' around. Y'hear? You gotta be my right-hand man. You gotta pull for me, 'cause I gotta be "head of household" now that Daddy's laid off. So get on over here an' gimme one a them Limey kisses I married you for. (*They kiss.*) Mmmmmmm . . . . I think we oughta forget breakfast and go right back to bed. (*Two rifle shots are heard. Joe reacts mildly.*) Uh-oh.

IRIS. What was that?

JOE. Daddy either got a rabbit . . . or old man Wiggins. (*Kisses her.*) I better go find out which. (*He exits.*)

IRIS. Don't leave me, Joe! Let me come with you!

JOE. You stay inside, Baby cakes. I don't want your backside peppered with buckshot . . . it belongs to me, now! Wheee-hooo! (*Pokes his head back in the door.*) Hey, I'll be workin' on the Buick if you need me. Daddy ran that thing into the ground while I was gone.

IRIS. (*To audience, examining her shoes for tarantulas.*) Poor bugger! I felt sorry for him over that car. That's mostly what he'd talked about in England, this big, pink Buick. It was soo.o..o long, he said, that when he parked it, the headlights were at one end of town and the taillights were at the other. Well, I soon found out that wasn't because the car was so long but because the bloody town was so short. (*She begins to unpack.*) Great big fins, he said, and leopard-skin seat covers and a radio with reverberating speakers in the back . . . and even a *lighter* for your cigarettes and everything. Well, *that's* a bit of Hollywood, right there, I thought, on wheels, or close enough. (*Puts clothing in the drawers.*) See, one thing you have to understand is how *grey* England was after the war. Grey. Everything. Bloody great yawning holes everywhere, piles of rubble. No colors. No nothing. Dead as a doornail. Talk about boring. (*Katrine opens the door. She is carrying a faded, long housedress and a babushka.*)

KATRINE. These clothes for workin' in. (*She lays housedress on the bed.*) Momma said to wear 'em.

IRIS. Anything else?

KATRINE. You wanna go to the outhouse . . . you gotta ask *me.*

IRIS. Why?

KATRINE. 'Cause you can't get by King by yourself.

IRIS. King?

KATRINE. That shepherd we got out there. We let it run. Keep the niggers outa our outhouse. Keep Wiggins outa the squash. That dog chew you right up. (*Pause.*) But *I* can get you by him.

IRIS. Thanks.

KATRINE. You can walk in heels like that?

IRIS. Yes. Like them?

KATRINE. Stupid.

IRIS. (*Anxious to make friends.*) I made one once, you know.

KATRINE. What?

IRIS. A shoe. Want to see it?

KATRINE. Yeah.

IRIS. (*Takes a high heel out of her case.*) See? I made the whole thing by meself.

KATRINE. Where's the other'n?

IRIS. I only made one.

KATRINE. Got two feet ain't ya?

IRIS. It's my *lucky* shoe. I take it everywhere with me.

KATRINE. Stupid.

IRIS. Well, you're entitled to your opinion, but this shoe made a big difference to my life. You might not believe it to look at me now, but I got thrown out of school when I was fifteen. Didn't even bother me the way it should have. I went right out and got a job on the glueing machine at Barrett's Shoe Shop. And do you know what happened, Kattie?

KATRINE. 'magine you gonna tell me.

25

IRIS. I got put in this government program. See, anybody under eighteen in a factory had to go to school one day a week to learn more about what they were slaving over. Can you imagine? (*Katrine shakes her head.*) We had to make a whole shoe from start to finish . . . even the design. And guess what the teacher did? He pinned *my* little drawing up on the blackboard and said: (*Affects upper-class accent.*) "Well done, Iris, beautifully drawn!" (*Rapidly.*) Well, I can't describe the feeling. I went red-hot . . . me whole body . . . to think I could do something . . . *well.* D'you understand? My shoe was the best one . . . put the heel on it meself and everything. I've never had a feeling of excitement quite like that again. Not even when I got married, Kattie. (*Wistfully.*) I've still got that shoe, though.
KATRINE. You talk too much.
IRIS. I thought you might be interested, that's all.
KATRINE. (*She sits on the bed.*) I was born in this bed.
IRIS. Were you?
KATRINE. This is *my* room.
IRIS. I know. I'm ever so sorry they took it away from you . . . honestly.
KATRINE. You can have it.
IRIS. (*Moved.*) That's very nice, Kattie. I'll look after everything, I promise.
KATRINE. Joe tol' Momma you brung me a present from England. What is it?
IRIS. (*Handing Katrine a package from suitcase.*) Why don't you open it and find out?
KATRINE. (*Opens it and takes out cheap charm bracelet.*) What's it for?
IRIS. It's a lucky charm bracelet. See! That one's the Houses of Parliament . . . that's Big Ben . . . and this one's a teeny-weeny teapot. Do you like it? (*Katrine hands present back.*) Well . . . I'll put it here on my dresser . . . I mean, *your* dresser . . . and if you change your mind . . .
KATRINE. I won't.
IRIS. All right.
KATRINE. I got sump'n for you. (*She takes a box from beneath her apron.*)
IRIS. Ohhh, Kattie . . . you shouldn't have.
KATRINE. I didn't wrap it.

26

IRIS. Never mind. It's the thought that counts, love. (*Katrine hands Iris the box.*) Shall I close me eyes while I take the top off?
KATRINE. No.
IRIS. (*Opens the box excitedly but drops it with a bloodcurdling scream.*) Aaaaaaaaa-aaaaaaagggggggggggggggghhhhhh. . . . Aaaaaaaaaagggggggggggggghhhhh. . . . (*Katrine runs out, Iris is hysterical. Joe hurries in.*)
JOE. Iris! Iris . . . what the hell is goin' on? What's wrong?
IRIS. Kattie . . . she . . .
JOE. Kattie? What?
IRIS. Over there . . . in . . . in the box . . .
JOE. Where? (*Finds it.*) Oh, for Chrissakes, Iris, it's just a prayin' mantis is all it is! *They don't even bite!* It's not dangerous. It's just a lousy *insect*, for cryin' out loud! (*He exits with the bug.*)
IRIS. (*To audience as she changes into the faded housedress.*) Well, that was the first time but it wasn't the last. I got used to her, though. I had to, didn't I? Mind you, I don't think she was near as daft as *they* thought she was. I had half a mind it was a sense of humor Kattie had got — a bit twisted — but a sense of humor just the same. Actually, she might have got along quite well in England . . . (*She ties the babushka on her head and looks comically forlorn and unlike herself.*) People like a practical joke or two where I come from. (*Lights fade.*)

ACT I

SCENE 3

A week later.
Lights come up in the kitchen. Joe is shaving at the sink. There are drawings of shoes taped to the Frigidaire. Stephan enters from outside with his gun wearing a red plaid hunting jacket and matching hat with ear-flaps.

JOE. Hey.
STEPHAN. (*Registers the shoe sketches as he opens the fridge.*) What happened to the goddamn vodka?
JOE. You drank it, Daddy.
STEPHAN. Shit! (*Slams fridge door.*) You speak to Janos like I tol' you?

27

JOE. Yep. Said we help him get that septic tank in, he'll trade us enough paint to spruce up this house for Momma.

STEPHAN. So . . . Hell, let's go!

JOE. I can't now.

STEPHAN. What? You gonna stick aroun', clean house for your wife?

JOE. Cut it out, Daddy.

STEPHAN. You gotta get that woman in line. She talks too damn much. A woman talks alla time ain't no good for work. She's sittin aroun' drawin' pictures while Momma's scrubbin' an'. . . .

JOE. She likes to draw shoes. What d'ya want me to do?

STEPHAN. I'm tellin' you, show her *now*, boy . . . if you wanna keep her. Your Momma kicked like a mule when I married her, too.

JOE. (*Laughs.*) High-spirited, huh?

STEPHAN. She's a good wife now.

JOE. Sure is.

STEPHAN. They don't come no better.

JOE. (*Teasing gently.*) Gettin' sentimental?

STEPHAN. Agghh . . . a man that hang aroun' the house twenty-four hours a day get soft in the head.

JOE. That what's happening to you, Daddy? (*Flicks him playfully with the towel.*) Huh? Huh?

STEPHAN. I can still whip your ass. (*They box around the table; Stephan ends up coughing.*)

JOE. Hey, . . . whyn't you go on up to Union Hall . . . talk to the guys?

STEPHAN. Talk! Talk! I talk there yesterday! I talk there this mornin'! I don't want to talk. I didn't get these scars on my back, this hole in my lung talkin'. I get 'em workin'. (*Marie enters with heavy coal bucket.*)

MARIE. We know. We know, Old Man.

STEPHAN. (*Smack's Marie's behind affectionately as she passes.*) Now, *that's* a worker.

MARIE. Lucky for you.

STEPHAN. (*Laughs and coughs.*) Agh, lessgo Sneaky Pete's, boy.

JOE. (*Sneaking the car keys into his pocket.*) Nah, I'm headed over the sawmill . . . they're lookin' for couple guys.

STEPHAN. Everybody's lookin' till you get there . . . then they ain't lookin' no more.

JOE. (*Flexing his muscles.*) I'm gettin' this one.

STEPHAN. Oh, yeah?

JOE. That guy Skuska owes me a favor. I'm tellin' ya . . . (*Great confidence.*) It's in the bag.

MARIE. He'll get sump'n, Daddy.

STEPHAN. He was gettin' sump'n in McKeesport, too. What did he get? He got nothin'.

JOE. How the hell's anybody gonna buy 'luminum sidin' when they can't pay the mortgage? It wasn't even wages, Daddy. Commission. Shit! You know them sellin' jobs sprout up faster than ragweed when there ain't no work.

STEPHAN. You coulda give it a try.

JOE. I ain't suckin' the blood outa the guy next door for no fly-by-night vacuum cleaner vultures.

MARIE. That's right.

JOE. Sump'n else'll come up.

STEPHAN. (*Coughing.*) I'm goin' beer garden. Gimme couple dollars, Marie. (*She gives him two, he waits for three.*) Where's the keys to the Buick? (*Marie signals a "no" to Joe.*)

JOE. Floorboards is rotted through. I gotta work on it. I'll drop you off.

STEPHAN. (*Grabs his jacket and gun.*) Forget it.

JOE. It ain't safe.

STEPHAN. Safe for you but not safe for me? You a better man than your father?

JOE. Aw, c'mon, Daddy . . .

STEPHAN. I can walk. (*Stephan exits slamming the screen door.*)

MARIE. Oi-yoi . . . he's gonna buy whiskey for them whore women.

JOE. Nah.

MARIE. If he's too drunk to dig for Janos, we ain't gonna get that paint for the house.

JOE. Hey . . . if he's too high, I'll dig it myself. (*He flexes his muscles.*)

MARIE. You big, strong man. I'm proud. You gotta good head, too. So use it. You be good to that wife.

JOE. Y'hear the bedsprings goin', don't ya?

MARIE. That coochie stuff wears off. There's got to be more.

You gotta learn to give l'il bit to a woman . . . from the heart. Pay attention. I know you want to make Daddy feel good but if the time come an' there ain't no work, you take your wife an' go.

JOE. Things gonna open up again real soon.

MARIE. But if they don't . . .

JOE. I ain't leavin' my family. I ain't my brother. An' I ain't endin' up like Pishta . . . my name off the list . . . whole damn family actin' like he's dead.

MARIE. Pishta was smart to go. Daddy knew his boy would go down that dirt road someday . . . always bullheaded . . . never two good words for his father. Not like you.

JOE. Pishta's wild as they come.

MARIE. That's the way your father was. He was gonna go out West, too, with his accordian . . . take the world by the shirttail. But you see . . . Pishta wasn't from Old Country. He didn't wanna stick around, kiss an ol' man's ass till he drop dead without a thank-you . . . the way *your* Daddy did for his Daddy. Back then a man owed first to the father and only then to his wife. I know. (*She sighs.*) No more. Pishta was right. Least I know he ain't down no mine.

JOE. You don't know where the hell he is. Sumbitch never wrote a line to you.

MARIE. Did *you* write? (*Painful pause.*) Same for your brother.

JOE. (*Jumping up.*) It's gonna be different now, Momma. I'm gonna make everything up to you an' Daddy. I'm gonna paint the house . . . get that Buick in shape. (*Kisses her cheek.*) An' I brung you home my l'il gooney-bird . . .

MARIE. Another mouth to feed.

JOE. I brung her special to cheer younse up.

MARIE. (*Pushes him away.*) Why you didn't bring me an ashtray like a normal son?

JOE. C'mon . . . how long's it been since you had another woman to talk to?

MARIE. (*Beat.*) You tell her anything?

JOE. What she don't know won't hurt her.

MARIE. She finds out, it's gonna hurt.

JOE. Nobody ain't tellin' nobody. It's all past. I'm home. Everything's gonna be fine. I'll *make* it fine!

MARIE. You good son. (*She picks up the heavy laundry basket.*)

JOE. Hey . . . lemme get that for ya. C'mon . . . C'mon . . .

30

(*Marie struggles vainly to keep the basket for a moment but finally relinquishes it. They exit laughing. Suddenly, there is a sound of footsteps running on the porch and a dog snarling. Iris dashes in, barely escaping the animal. She slams the door and leans against it to catch her breath.*)
IRIS. (*To audience.*) Ooooohhh . . . that blinkin' dog! (*Beat.*) Wellllll . . . I'd made *some* headway. At least, he'd learned to let me *in* the outhouse . . . just hadn't learned to bloody-well let me *out* yet!
JOE'S VOICE. That you, Iris?
IRIS. Yes!
JOE. (*Entering.*) Hey, that man-eatin' mutt scare you to death?
IRIS. He's not exactly Rin-Tin-Tin, is he? (*They laugh.*)
JOE. Momma says I'm neglectin' you. That right?
IRIS. I don't see much of you, do I?
JOE. You been tellin' her I don't give you nothin'?
IRIS. Is that what she told you?
JOE. (*Picks her up and swings her around.*) I give you a baby, didn't I?
IRIS. Oh, very generous.
JOE. An' I give you a nice, red telephone. Anybody ever give you a telephone before?
IRIS. Never!
JOE. (*Puts her down.*) Then why ain't you used it?
IRIS. I don't know anybody to call.
JOE. Call the operator.
IRIS. Don't be daft.
JOE. I wanna see you use it. Go on! Dial zero.
IRIS. What shall I say?
JOE. Ask her what time is it. She's gonna shit, she hears that English accent.
IRIS. (*Dials.*) Hello . . . operator? I wonder if you could tell me the time . . . 1:32PM . . . thank you very much . . . England . . .
JOE. What'd I tell ya!
IRIS. Sssssshhhhh . . . (*To operator.*) Just a couple of weeks, actually . . .
JOE. (*His ear to the phone, too.*) Tell her I put you in a red phone.
IRIS. Well . . . I'm not sure . . . I haven't really seen anything . . . no . . . I haven't been off the estate yet . . . the chauffeur's been a bit busy . . . no . . . no, not so far . . . yes . . . well, the language thing's a bit difficult, isn't it? I mean, it's the same

31

words but sometimes the meanings are different. What? . . .
well, I can't think of an example at the moment.

JOE. (*Thoroughly enjoying himself.*) Tell her about the pecker . . .
the chin . . . you know!

IRIS. (*Whispering*) Noooooo, silly.

JOE. Go on! She don't know who the hell she's talkin' to.

IRIS. No . . . me husband . . . reminding me of one of those
different meanings . . . it's a little bit rude, actually . . . Well,
you see, in England, a slang word for chin . . . *chin* . . . is. . . .

JOE. *Tell her* . . . pecker!

IRIS. Is, ahhmm . . . pecker. (*Giggles.*) Yes, I know . . . caused
quite a muck-up when us English girls when round telling the
Yanks to keep their peckers up . . . meaning *chin*, of course . . .
Right! . . . disastrous results . . . population explosion . . .
(*Whispers to Joe.*) She's laughing her head off . . . Well, thank
you, operator . . . Iris . . . what's yours? . . . Elvira-Mae? . . .
Ooohhh, that's very unusual, isn't it? . . . Yes, p'raps I will . . .
Well, cheerio.

JOE. (*Laughing hysterically.*) Cheee-ree-ho! (*He hangs the phone
up.*) You know why I married you?

IRIS. (*Pats her pregnant belly.*) Haven't got a clue.

JOE. 'Cause you make me laugh. (*He hugs her.*) An' I ain't never
gonna let you get away. Never. (*They kiss.*)

IRIS. You mean that, Joe?

JOE. I do.

IRIS. (*Urgently.*) Then let me come with you now.

JOE. I can't, hon . . .

IRIS. Please, Joe. Let me come for the ride.

JOE. I gotta look for work. I can't drag my wife. I'll get laughed
at.

IRIS. I can't stay in this house anymore, miles from nowhere. I
want to do something! I want to see something! (*He breaks
away.*) After you come back, will you take me?

JOE. (*Puts his jacket on.*) Soon's I get a job, I'll take you to the
mountains or sump'n.

IRIS. I don't want to see a mountain. I want to go to Woolworth's.

JOE. (*Heads to the door.*) C'mon, Iris . . . go find Momma . . .
see them quilts on the beds. She made every damn one by hand.
She'll teach you how to do it.

IRIS. (*Runs after him.*) I hate sewing.

JOE. Try an' cheer, Momma up, OK? Tell her about the pecker.

IRIS. I can't tell your mother things like *that*!

JOE. Sure you can. (*Grabs his cap.*) She needs a couple jokes, kid. She's had it rough. Now don't you go to sleep before I get home, y'hear? (*Smooches her neck.*) I want you all pink an' sweet-smellin' in that lace thing I got ya . . . propped up on them goose-down ticks like a l'il English bird in a feather nest.

IRIS. Ohh, Joe . . . that's all you think of.

JOE. I gotta get me plenty a' practise. (*He exits.*) I want ten. Ten kids.

JOE'S VOICE. (*Hollering to all in Willard Patch.*) All boys! Wheeeeehooooo!

IRIS. (*Staring after him.*) Ten? One down . . . only nine to go. (*She stares around her for a moment and then sneaks to the telephone, dials.*) Hello? . . . Elvira-mae . . . Oh, it *is* you . . . yes . . . the English one . . . Iris . . . (*Lowers her voice.*) I . . . ahhmm . . . wanted to ask you something . . . see, me husband teases me a bit . . . he says it's *3,000* miles to California. Is that true?

MARIE'S VOICE. *Iris!* Bring dustpan!

IRIS. Coming! (*To Elvira-Mae.*) Well, how much does it cost to get there? . . . Bus, I suppose . . . Oh, just me and me husband . . . Well, better make it three . . . four if I have twins. (*She laughs but stops abruptly.*) *That* much? God, you need to be King Farouk to go anywhere here . . .

MARIE'S VOICE. *III . . . rrisss!*

IRIS. Ooh, I've got to go . . . no . . . thanks everso . . . Cheerio, Elvira-Mae . . . yes . . . I'd like to meet you, as well . . . someday. Ta-ta. (*She hangs up.*) Blimey . . . (*She addresses the audience as she ties a babushka over her hair.*) Still, the way I looked at it was this: nobody had clunked me over the head and dragged me off to America in a coma, had they? I'd made me bed . . . (*Puts apron on.*) And till I'd sorted out what to do next . . . it was up to me to learn how to lie in it.

MARIE'S VOICE. *IIIII . . . rrisss!!* There's work to do!

IRIS. (*Fetches dustpan.*) Easier said than done. Honestly, I'd never seen anyone slave like those women in Willard Patch. (*On her way to the door, she pauses to look at a shoe drawing taped to the fridge door.*) I'm telling you, up at the crack of dawn every bloody day, filling up their buckets with little scraps of coal from the slag heap. Scrub, scrub, scrubbing . . . sweep, sweep, sweeping away at the old coal dust. (*She reaches on top of the fridge for more drawings.*) I couldn't keep up with them. (*Wanders absentmindedly to the table.*) Well, between you and me and the bedpost, in my delicate condition, I didn't exactly break me neck trying. (*She sits. Hungarian music starts softly.*) Besides, I was too busy trying to perfect a new batch of shoe designs I'd dreamed up. (*Iris begins drawing. Lights fade. The music takes over.*)

ACT I

SCENE 4

A few weeks later. Kitchen. Iris is drawing shoes. The table is littered with crayons and paper. Her lucky shoe is standing on an upturned mixing bowl. Tacked to the wall beside her are a couple of elaborate shoe designs. Marie is working at the stove. It is early morning.

IRIS. I wrote into "Queen For A Day" and told them I had a terminal illness and wanted to die in California.
MARIE. Ssshhhh . . . don't let Daddy hear that.
IRIS. (*Examining her design critically.*) They never even wrote back.
MARIE. Aghh, they got deaf and blind women with twelve kids that don't even win. Oi-yoi-yoi-yoi . . . (*A sudden sadness descends on her. She turns to Iris.*) So much trouble in the world, Iris.
IRIS. Want to hear a joke, Mrs. Kovacs?
MARIE. I used to like a good joke.
IRIS. See, the Duke of Bedford met Lord Chumley at his club one day. And the Duke says: "Sorry, old chap, I hear you buried your wife." And Lord Chumley says: "Had to, old boy . . . *dead*, you know!" (*Iris laughs uproariously at her own joke, and resumes drawing.*)
MARIE. We don't make fun of the dead here.
IRIS. In England we do.
MARIE. Come put your husband's breakfast on the table.
IRIS. Can I just finish this? (*Holds up drawing.*) See . . . round

34

the ankle? It's got these transparent straps with little diamonds trapped inside. (*Stephan enters, carrying a rifle.*) Ohh . . . 'morning, Mr. Kovacs (*Marie hands him coffee.*) Did you have a nice sleep?

STEPHAN. (*He stares at her for a long moment, speaks gruffly but not loud.*) You learn to make bread yet?

IRIS. Ahhm . . . no . . . not yet.

STEPHAN. You learn to make goulash?

IRIS. Well, not quite . . . it's getting there, though.

JOE'S VOICE. (*From bedroom.*) Iris?

IRIS. What?

JOE'S VOICE. I can't find any goddamn socks!

IRIS. You'll have to put your yesterday ones on, then.

JOE'S VOICE. Jeezus H. Christ . . . (*Joe and Katrine enter simultaneously through different doors. Katrine hands him a freshly-ironed shirt with a competitive glance at Iris.*)

STEPHAN. Some wife you got . . . no socks . . . no goulash. You gonna die starvation in your bare feet. (*He exits out to the porch. Joe stares after him, humiliated by Iris's incompetence.*)

JOE. (*To Iris.*) I ain't got all day you know. (*Katrine gives him clean socks from her apron pocket.*)

IRIS. Are you going to Welfare?

JOE. That's right! Holler "Welfare", so Daddy hears.

IRIS. (*Loud whisper.*) How long will you be?

JOE. Depends how many people in line.

IRIS. Can I come with you?

JOE. No.

MARIE. (*Buttoning Joe's shirt.*) What happened with the job you went for yesterday?

JOE. Same thing happened with the sawmill. Same damn thing happened with all the others. (*He sits at the table.*)

IRIS. Did they take your name down?

JOE. (*Puts socks on.*) What'd they want with my fuckin' name? They got hundreds a' names.

IRIS. I just wondered. (*Katrine hands him his boots. Marie signals Iris frantically, behind Joe's back, to pour him coffee. To Marie.*) Ohhh . . . (*To Joe.*) Would you like some coffee?

JOE. Yeah.

IRIS. (*Hangs towel comically over her arm like a waiter and pours.*) Joe?

JOE. What?

IRIS. Do you know what today is?

JOE. Wednesday.

IRIS. What else?

JOE. What, for Chrissakes?

IRIS. Don't you know?

JOE. No.

IRIS. It's the anniversary of something very special that happened nineteen years ago in England. (*Marie puts his breakfast on the table.*) You know what you are, Iris?

JOE. You know what you are, Iris?

IRIS. What? (*She lavishly salts and peppers his eggs.*)

JOE. Nuts!

IRIS. Getting a bit free with the compliments, aren't we?

MARIE. (*Hands him the bread.*) Don't call your wife names.

JOE. You know anyone else who hauls around *one* high-heeled shoe?

IRIS. I happen to be very proud of this shoe.

JOE. Do I have to have it on my damn table?

IRIS. It's all I've got left of England.

JOE. Uh-oh . . . here we go with England again. Christ. (*Beat.*) You wanna know what we shoulda done?

IRIS. I don't want to hear one more time how some G.I. should have pulled the plug out of England and sunk it. It's not funny.

JOE. Shoulda done it myself.

IRIS. Take more than a Yank to sink us. The Germans couldn't do it and they're intelligent.

JOE. You know how much England owes this country?

MARIE. Oi-yoi-yoi-yoi . . . you beginnin' to sound like Daddy.

JOE. Least my old man knows what the hell he's talkin' about . . . not like her.

MARIE. (*Pulling Katrine with her, she exits.*) C'mon, Pitcher with Big Ears . . . back to the ironin'. (*Iris and Joe stare defiantly at each other across the table. Her inability to understand the loss of manhood that goes with unemployment and his inadequacy to tell her what's really wrong, create a painful tension. Iris, finally, gives in. She reaches her hand to him.*)

IRIS. Oh, Joe . . . I wish we wouldn't argue so much.

JOE. (*Ignores her outstretched hand.*) Quit startin' it, then.

IRIS. You're getting ever so mean.

36

JOE. It ain't me. It's you. You hate this country.

IRIS. No. I'm homesick, that's all. People didn't take themselves so seriously in England. *We* didn't take ourselves seriously. Ohh, Lovie, remember that night, on top of the old number nine bus? We missed our stop we were laughing so hard.

JOE. I remember.

IRIS. Why aren't we like that now?

JOE. 'Cause you keep doin' *this* shit. (*He stabs at her drawings.*) I don't want you drawin' shoes no more.

IRIS. Why?

JOE. You're supposed to be my wife.

IRIS. What's that make me? The Prisoner of Zenda? I've got to have something. I'm withering away! I'm turning into a cabbage.

JOE. Cut it out.

IRIS. I never see you.

JOE. Cut it out!

IRIS. It's no wonder I can't make your Mum laugh. I can't remember how to laugh meself.

JOE. (*Shouts.*) I said: Cut It Out! (*Pause. He suddenly reaches out and takes her hand.*) Look . . . I know it ain't easy. You think I got it any better, kid? Just hold on. I'll find work. I'll get you some nice things for the baby. We'll be OK.

IRIS. Will we, Joe?

JOE. (*Gets up and moves away.*) It's just that Pennsylvania is the worst place to be right now. We're in a recession . . . s'all mines an' shut-down steel mills here an' . . .

IRIS. Is it?

JOE. What?

IRIS. The *worst* place?

JOE. For jobs? Bottom of the barrel.

IRIS. (*Excited.*) Well, we're all right, then!

JOE. How y'mean?

IRIS. Well, if this is the *worst* place . . . everywhere else in America is *better*, right? We could move! We could, Joe. Any place we went, it would be an improvement. We can't make a mistake, can we? We'll just move . . . maybe California . . . (*She runs to him, hugs him.*) *California,* Duckie!

JOE. How the hell we gonna move on welfare money?

IRIS. I'll clean houses or something.

JOE. Who's gonna pay *you* to clean house? You don't know your ass from your elbow 'bout keepin' house.

IRIS. I'll learn.

JOE. (*He surveys her mess on the table.*) You won't *never* learn.

IRIS. Then why did you marry me?

JOE. Used to be nice . . . used to look nice. See you now? Like some damn ol' woman in that rag.

IRIS. Oh, this is a present from your side of the family. I'd sew a few sequins on it, if I thought they could stand the excitement.

JOE. (*Snatches his jacket up.*) Look like a pregnant scarecrow . . .

IRIS. You're the one put me in this condition.

JOE. (*Quietly.*) Far as I know.

IRIS. Oh, that's nice.

JOE. How's any guy know he's the father?

IRIS. Is that what your Dad said?

JOE. S'true, ain't it?

IRIS. If you had any doubts, Joe Kovacs, you didn't have to . . .

JOE. Yeah . . . I bet you never did love me. That's right. You was just lookin' for some sucker to give you an easy life.

IRIS. Easy life?

JOE. Thought you was gonna live high off the hog in Willard, didn't ya?

IRIS. O, yes . . . mecca of entertainment . . . fifteen houses, a petrol pump and one shop that sells everything from Kotex to horse feed.

JOE. You got more'n you ever had. You think my Mom had TV an' her own telephone when she got married?

IRIS. Your Mum. I think you picked me up for a souvenir for your Mum.

JOE. Bullshit!

IRIS. Somebody to help with the chores . . . somebody to be just like her.

JOE. You'll never be like my mother. You couldn't never go through what she's been through an' come out in one piece.

IRIS. You're right. I'd be gone right round the bend, hanging off the side of a coal mine for fifty years.

JOE. (*Tears her sketches from the wall.*) You don't even care if I bust my balls tryin' a' find work just for you.

IRIS. Don't! Don't!

JOE. Well, you ain't wastin' anymore a my time . . . (*He grabs her lucky shoe.*)

IRIS. (*Screams.*) No . . . not my shoe!

JOE. You think more a this goddamn thing than you do a me, don't ya? (*He holds the shoe up out of her reach.*) Don't ya?

IRIS. (*Struggling to get it.*) No. No.

JOE. Don't ya?

IRIS. Yes! Yes, I do!

JOE. Well, now you can file for divorce! (*He throws the shoe in the coal stove.*)

IRIS. (*Softly but intense.*) I would if I had the money.

JOE. You ain't gonna leave me, Iris. I . . .

IRIS. Don't touch me!

JOE. Well, you can try leavin', kid, if you wanna see the wrong end a that gun in there.

IRIS. Just go.

JOE. They'd take one look at the fruitcake I married, I wouldn't even have to go to jail. Now, if you don't mind . . . (*Pushes her aside.*) I gotta go sweep Daisyville streets for your welfare check.

IRIS. You bastard. (*He slaps her face and slams out. She runs to the screen door and yells after him.*) It's my rotten birthday today! My nineteenth birthday! A birthday is a big thing in England . . . because it's a *civilized* country . . . not like *this* pox-eaten coal mine. I'm not going to be a servant! I'm going to be an artist! (*Tearfully.*) And I didn't even get a birthday card from Freda . . . nor you, you . . . (*Yells out again.*) You big, dumb, Hungarian-Polack. And don't think I'll be here when you get back, neither. *I'm* going to California . . . you see if I don't! (*She runs sobbing to the bedroom and begins packing wildly at first but soon runs out of steam. To the audience.*) I must've cried for hours. Even thought of killing meself. I reckoned it would serve the old bugger right, if he came home and found me hanging in the old two-holer with me eyes bulging out a mile and a note to Freda pinned to me arse saying: "This corpse is a British citizen and proud of it. Please ship to it's country of origin." But I soon chucked that idea. I mean, it wouldn't have been fair to old Freda, would it? And there was a baby to consider. (*Marie enters the bedroom followed by Katrine who has a red dress over her arm. Marie carries some envelopes.*)

39

MARIE. Come, now . . . don't be so foolish . . . (*She takes things out of the suitcase.*) Joe's got a hard time. (*Iris puts them back in.*) What do you know the shame a man feels with no work? (*Takes clothes back out.*) He wants to be a good husband. He don't know how yet. Like you don't know how to be a good wife.

IRIS. He burned my shoe . . . my lucky shoe.

MARIE. What luck? You make your own luck. Kattie! (*Forces a card on Katrine.*) Give her the birthday mail. See? One from me an' one from Kattie . . . an' one from Joe . . .

KATRINE. *You* bought that.

MARIE. An' one from Eng-a-land . . .

IRIS. (*Excited.*) From Freda? It is! (*Tears it open quickly.*)

MARIE. What she say? Read.

IRIS. "Dear Twit . . ."

MARIE. Twit?

IRIS. That's what she calls me . . . "Count your blessings on your birthday. I miss you. Your pal forever, Freda. P.S. Keep your pecker up!"

MARIE. There, you see? Count the blessings . . . keep up with the pecker!

IRIS. (*Tearfully.*) Oh, I miss her. I miss her so much.

MARIE. Sometime, we have to leave friends behind. (*She hands Iris the other cards.*) Now open . . . mine got the X.X.X.'s, see? An' I made a heart on Joe's.

IRIS. Oh, Mrs. Kovacs. (*She kisses Marie's cheek.*) Thanks ever so . . .

KATRINE. She ain't your mother. She's mine.

MARIE. Big ox . . . gimme that dress! Look, Iris, what I got for you. Pretty? (*She holds up a very large, matronly, chiffon cocktail dress.*) Joe won't call you scarecrow again, he sees you in this. You think this dumb, ol' Hunky ain't been nowhere? Ain't seen nothin'? Look at this fancy-dancy. You like?

IRIS. Ummhh . . . ahhh, well . . . it's very . . . unusual . . .

KATRINE. She *forced* me get that card.

MARIE. Put it on. (*Assists Iris into the dress.*) Once when Stephan was on strike, I went to New York. That surprise you, huh? I went to clean house for Jew-woman. But she don't treat me like no house-keep. I was one of the family. Always they say: "Marie, you so smart! Marie, you so talented! Take this

40

dress. Marie, there ain't nobody in the world make bread like you! Take another dress." They was in the dress business. Kattie, hand me pins! (*She helps Iris up onto a chair.*) Anything I want they give me . . . just so I stay. I got closet full of dresses you wouldn't believe. (*She kneels.*)

IRIS. You should wear them.

MARIE. (*Swiftly pinning the hem.*) What? I'm going to have people say: "Where did Marie get such fancies? Marie must be a you-know-what!" But sometime I look in the closet, you know . . . (*The memory brings a gentleness to her voice.*) feel the silk in my hand . . . then I feel good. There . . . I pinned up the hem. (*She stands.*)

IRIS. (*Examining her bulging tummy in the ill-fitting dress.*) It's a little bit big I think.

MARIE. Soooo . . . you eat right . . . you'll grow into it. Now . . . what did I tell to say, Katrine?

KATRINE. I ain't sayin' it!

MARIE. Say it!

KATRINE. No!

MARIE. (*Slaps Katrine.*) I said: Say it!

KATRINE. (*Murderously.*) Happy Birthday!

END OF ACT I

ACT II

A few months later. Early spring.
The stage is in total darkness. A spotlight comes up on Iris
seated in a rocking chair Down Stage Right. Her face is well
scrubbed and her hair is drawn neatly back with a ribbon. The
baby is due and she seems to have acquired a new maturity. She
is knitting.

IRIS. England started to fade from me mind after a while. I
could hardly remember what a good plate of fish and chips
tasted like. MMmmmmmmm . . . fish and chips. (*Nostalgic
sigh.*) And you know what? With every inch me waistline ex-
panded, California seemed to get less important and further
away. Funny how you change, isn't it? Getting to the baby
counter at Woolworth's became more of a challenge than getting to Hollywood. Still, it wasn't *all* bad. I remember the trees
caught fire with colors enough to break your bloody heart that
year. I wrote and told Freda about it. All red and gold. Brighter
than any sequins old Doris Day ever got pasted into. I'd never
seen an autumn like that. Even bleedin' Willard Patch looked
pretty for a couple of weeks. The men came and went with guns
and dead animals and car parts, grumbling about jobs and foot-
ball. The days passed. And when the winter came, great prison
bars of icicles grew over the windows. Well . . . they used to call
pregnancy a confinement, didn't they? What else could I do? I
just settled in to watch me belly grow. That part was nice. I liked
being pregnant. It was like having a secret all me own . . . or a
present coming in the post. Something brand new and in-
teresting to look forward to. (*Confidentially.*) Mind you, Kattie
still ran me a dog's life and the old man avoided me like the pox,
but after that knock-down-drag-out with Joe on my birthday,
Marie seemed to warm up to me a bit. I didn't know why. But I
was ever so glad. (*She exits.*)

ACT II

Scene 1

Early spring. Lights come up in the kitchen. The folding screen
stands, extended, Upstage. Signs of bread-making on the table.
Marie with flour up to her wrists is on the telephone. Katrine is

noisily filling the stove with coal. Marie shouts to make herself heard.

MARIE. Marie Kovacs . . . that's right . . . I'm callin' 'bout job application Stephan Kovacs put in . . . We didn't hear nothin' yet . . . yeah, I'll wait . . . (*To Katrine.*) Enough with that noise, I'm tryin' to talk.

KATRINE. (*Spitefully.*) How come the Johnny Bull don't pick coal when we go?

MARIE. Leave her alone. She got lifetime to pick coal. (*Into telephone.*) Yeah, I'm still here . . . how old? . . .

KATRINE. Fifty-nine.

MARIE. Sssshhh . . . (*Into phone.*) So you got it on the paper, so don't ask! . . . That ain't old . . . He's strong as a bull . . . you're gonna tell me he can't put up a few damn fences . . . yeah, yeah, yeah . . . you know what, Billy Tzerzinski, you was dumb when you went to school with my Joe an' you still dumb. I hope your old man's business goes bust . . . I hope your dog dies! (*She bangs receiver down and resumes bread-making.*) Oi-yoi-yoi-yoi. (*Dog starts barking.*)

IRIS. (*Entering with difficulty from outside.*) Get back, King. Back! (*Dog snarls viciously.*)

MARIE. (*Grabs a bone from stove and goes to the door.*) Throw him a bone, Iris. (*Marie throws bone out.*) Chew on that, you dumb mutt!

IRIS. He's doing quite well, actually. He lets me *in* and *out* of the outhouse now.

MARIE. Takes time. Pretty soon he's gonna figure out you live here.

IRIS. He let me sit by the fence and draw this morning, Mrs. Kovacs.

MARIE. Why you don't call me Mamma?

IRIS. I'd feel silly.

MARIE. Why?

IRIS. Only babies say "Mamma" and "Daddy" where I come from.

MARIE. (*Uncomfortable pause.*) OK . . . so you call me Marie.

IRIS. Want to see what I drew . . . Mrs. . . . Marie? (*She takes a drawing from her pocket.*)

MARIE. Flowers now? You don't draw shoes no more?

43

IRIS. I thought it was time for a change. Do you like it?

MARIE. You make nice pictures. Someday you make picture of me with my bread.

IRIS. (*Pinning up drawing of wildflower.*) Took me ever such a long time to get it right.

MARIE. Sure, you think I make good bread in five minutes?

IRIS. I wish I could be a real artist and lie in the sun and draw all day. (*Marie snorts contemptuously.*) I saw something on the back of a matchbook the other day. It says if you send in a sketch and they like it, you can get lessons free.

MARIE. Nothin' ain't free.

IRIS. I'd like to get a book on drawing.

MARIE. Nothin' round here.

IRIS. P'raps at Woolworth's?

MARIE. (*Sternly.*) We don't need to look in windows when there ain't no money to spend. Now come, I show you how to make the bread.

IRIS. I don't really like cooking.

MARIE. It don't matter what a wife like to do. It's what she got to do. Roll up your sleeves.

IRIS. (*Reluctantly rolls up her sleeves.*) Don't you ever like to do anything else, Marie? You know, apart from work?

MARIE. Sleep. At the end of the day, ain't nothin' look so good to me as my bed.

IRIS. But don't you like to read or anything? I love to read. You haven't even got any newspapers . . . not in English, anyway. (*Katrine ties a babushka on Iris's head to keep hair out of the dough.*)

MARIE. We don't bother.

IRIS. Why not?

MARIE. We stop takin' when Joe went in the service. He's the only one could read, so what's the use to keep payin'. Now wash the hands good, Iris. There ain't nothin' in them papers, anyways . . . divorce . . . stealin' . . .

KATRINE. Murder.

MARIE. (*Harshly.*) Make coffee! *Move!* (*Pause.*) What you see in that readin' stuff anyways, honey?

IRIS. Well, you find out what's going on, don't you? (*Washing hands.*) You learn about different people . . . and places . . . oh, God, do you think I'll ever get to California?

44

KATRINE. Pishta went there.

MARIE. Hush. (*To Iris.*) It ain't no use to make yourself crazy. Where the husband lives, that's where the wife lives. That's the way it is. Don't even talk about West. Oi-yoi . . . when my oldest boy ran off there . . . it was like he died for Daddy.

KATRINE. You ain't s'posed to talk about him.

MARIE. Joe's all Daddy got now. And grandson maybe under that shirt.

IRIS. I'd like a girl.

MARIE. Pray for a boy. A worker. Someone to help when you are old. Come, Iris. It's time to put the hands in the dough. You watch me, you won't need no measure. You see with the eyes, you weigh with the hands, you *feel* when it's right. (*Iris plunges her hands into the pan.*) You punch it down like this . . . see? No, no . . . not too hard. Like a man . . . you handle it *just* so. That's right! (*They laugh at the sexual reference.*) Now, don't it feel beautiful to your hands?

STEPHAN. (*Entering, pathetic without his job, unshaven.*) Buncha hens cacklin' down here.

MARIE. What's the matter, Daddy? You couldn't sleep?

STEPHAN. Sleep. That's all I do is sleep.

MARIE. Look, Daddy . . . you daughter-in-law . . . makin' bread . . .

STEPHAN. Marie . . . (*He draws her aside.*) That place call? About the job?

MARIE. Which?

STEPHAN. (*Urgent.*) With the fences. The job puttin' fences.

MARIE. Yeah.

STEPHAN. Well?

MARIE. (*Reluctantly.*) No good, Istvan.

STEPHAN. Hell with 'em!

MARIE. But listen you shoulda heard that guy. That's the best damn application, he says . . . (*Rhapsodizes.*) What kinda service . . . how many years . . . they never seen that kind experience you got, Daddy.

STEPHAN. (*Puts his jacket on.*) So why they didn't take me?

MARIE. Next time they're hirin', you're the first one they gonna call.

STEPHAN. Sure . . . (*Picks up his gun, speaks privately so Iris won't hear.*) Gimme couple dollars, Marie. (*Marie gives him two dollars discreetly from her apron pocket. He waits for more.*)

MARIE. You said couple. (*Reluctantly gives him another bill.*) Now don't stay too long. Don't get drunk! (*She buttons his coat lovingly.*) And don't start with Wiggins!

STEPHAN. He don't start with me, I don't start with him. (*He takes his gun and leaves.*)

MARIE. Oi-yoi-yoi . . . (*Turning away to hide her tears.*)

IRIS. Keep your pecker up, Marie.

MARIE. Sure.

IRIS. (*A pause.*) You know what you need?

MARIE. What?

IRIS. A good time. Don't people ever get together here?

MARIE. (*Blowing her nose.*) Together?

IRIS. To enjoy themselves.

MARIE. Oh, sure for wedding . . . for funeral. For funeral I make food you wouldn't believe.

IRIS. I was thinking of something a bit more lively, actually. In England, nearly every night, we stop in the pub . . . have a couple of pints.

MARIE. Pub?

IRIS. Like a bar.

MARIE. You drink with men?

IRIS. And women. Young and old. We all drink together. Play a bit of darts . . . have a good old sing-song.

MARIE. Daddy would put me outa my misery if I drink with men. There's some women does, with them blouses you can see all the way through. But not me! Oi-yoi-yoi . . . I wouldn't live to see the next day.

IRIS. You'd like it in England. We have such a good laugh.

MARIE. Yeah?

IRIS. Everybody gets up at the piano, with their pint, and does a turn. You should see me when I get going. Do you want to see?

MARIE. Boy-oh-boy . . . you gonna turn this house upside down.

IRIS. C'mon. (*Gets into the spirit.*) Let's have a laugh! Let me do you a turn! C'mon! (*She leaves the bread and grabs a feather duster.*) It'll only take a minute. Have you got a hat?

MARIE. Daddy's huntin' cap.

46

IRIS. That'll do. (*Sticks hunting cap, with earmuffs turned down, on her head.*) Sit down, everybody!

KATRINE. She's gonna get us in trouble.

IRIS. Are you ready!?!! (*Affects British music hall style.*) My Lords, ladies, and gentle. .m. .m. .en! That naughty lady of the music hall stage . . . I.rriss . . . Ko . . . vacs! Tatatatatah . . . Tatatatatahhh . . . Tah . . . Dah . . . (*Sings jauntily using feather duster for cane.*)

WHERE DID YOU GET THAT HAT? WHERE
   DID YOU GET THAT TILE?
ISN'T IT A LOVELY ONE, AND JUST THE
   PROPER STYLE!
I SHOULD LIKE TO HAVE ONE JUST THE SAME
   AS THAT!
WHERE E'ER I'D GO, THEY'D SHOUT "HELLO!"
(*Tap dance step.*)
WHERE DID YOU GET THAT HAT?
(*Rousing finale. Iris reappears for coda.*)
I SHOULD LIKE TO HAVE ONE JUST THE SAME
   AS THAT!
WHERE E'ER I'D GO, THEY'D SHOUT
   "HELL . . O . . O . . O!"
(*Throws hat into the air.*)
WHERE DID YOU GET THAT HAT?
(*Exits music-hall style into the closet.*)
GET ORF ME BARROW!
HAVE A BANANA!
WHERE DID YOU GET THAT HAAAT!

MARIE. (*Laughing.*) Oohh . . . oohhh . . . funny girl . . . Oh, I used to be like that, too. When I was young, with the Czardas . . . what a dancer I was. . . . No more. Oh, my, I was crazy too, like you . . . and thin . . . like a twig . . . my God . . . (*She drifts off into memory.*)

KATRINE. She got us behind on the chores, now.

MARIE. So . . . we go! (*She gets up.*) Oh, boy-oh-boy-oh-boy . . . that sure put the juice back in *my* batteries. OK, Iris, now back to the bread . . . Katrine, bring dustmop! (*Marie exits.*)

IRIS. Oh, Kattie. . . . wasn't that a scream? Who needs Hollywood, eh, Duckie? We'll call ourselves the "Wild Willard Wenches" and entertain all the pickers over on the old slag

47

heap. What d'you think?

KATRINE. (*Dangerously.*) She's *my* mother. She *ain't your'n.*

IRIS. I'm not going to take her away from you.

KATRINE. That's right.

IRIS. We can share her, Kattie.

KATRINE. Leave her alone.

IRIS. But I like her. What's wrong with that?

KATRINE. You wouldn't like her if you knew what she done.

IRIS. What do you mean?

KATRINE. She done sump'n bad so you better stay away from her.

IRIS. She hasn't done anything bad.

KATRINE. Wanna bet?

IRIS. What?

KATRINE. Sump'n.

IRIS. What?

KATRINE. Sump'n.

IRIS. Tell me!

KATRINE. She killed a man.

IRIS. What a terrible thing to say.

KATRINE. Shot him dead.

IRIS. I don't believe you.

KATRINE. Ask her.

IRIS. No wonder Joe smacks you. You're a naughty, jealous girl! You deserve it.

KATRINE. I don't tell lies. (*She goes to the dresser and gets a yellowed newspaper, gives it to Iris.*) It's in the paper . . . an' a picture a' Momma.

IRIS. Where? (*Snatches paper. Sees photograph.*) Oh, God . . . it *is* Marie . . . it *is!*

KATRINE. So better quit hangin' on her. Else she'll get you, too. (*Iris examines paper.*) Go on . . . read it!

IRIS. Mrs. Marie Kovacs is supported down the steps of the county courthouse, following her arraignment after the shooting death of coal miner Dan Krutchik . . . Oh, God . . . she really did. She really killed someone.

KATRINE. That's why Joe went into the service. Him an' Pishta seen it. I didn't get to see it.

IRIS. But why? Why did she?

48

KATRINE. (*Secretively.*) I got raped. Don't you tell Momma I tol'.

IRIS. You got raped?

KATRINE. (*With poignant simplicity.*) Sumabitch got off with it, Daddy said, 'cause the judge ask me was it snowin' when it happened an' I said yes. I forgot it was summer bein' I had my coat on. My head don't always work too good. Daddy was mad, boy, when he seen the blood . . .

IRIS. Blood?

KATRINE. It got on my Sunday apron . . . then that judge let the Hunky go. That's why we can't go in town. Daddy kep' sayin' he was gonna kill him . . . kep' settin' on the porch cussin' every day, sayin' how he's gonna get that raper if the law don't. 'I'll kill him! I'll kill him!' He kep' on sayin' it, but he didn't.

IRIS. What happened?

KATRINE. One day that Krutchik come offa his shift at the mine, an' Daddy's waitin' on the porch swing to go nex' shift, an' he's rockin' an' bangin' his dinner bucket . . . so you could hear it clear in the house. Momma took the bread out the oven and set it nice to cool . . .then she pick up that rifle an' went to the screen door. "You quit that bangin', now, Stephen." An' Daddy yell, "There goes that no good Hunky sumbitch. One day I'll blow his head off." (*Pause.*) So that's when Momma done it. Then she come back an' put the lard on the bread so the crust shine . . .

IRIS. (*Deeply shocked.*) That's awful.

KATRINE. Well, you got to put grease on the crust else it don't cut nice. (*Pause.*) Police let Momma take the bread over the neighborwoman's. Momma don't like no waste. (*She goes back to kitchen.*)

IRIS. (*Follows Katrine.*) But she's not in prison . . .

KATRINE. (*Sadly.*) She got sick in the head . . . like me. They let her go. I didn't like it when she wasn't here. (*Goes to screen door.*) Iris, you better cover that dough with a wet rag. (*Gently.*) She'll rise up on us, if you don't wet her down. (*She smiles with genuine sweetness. It is the first smile she's ever given to Iris. She leaves. After a moment, Marie enters carrying broom and dusters. Iris freezes.*)

MARIE. (*Cheerfully.*) Oh, Boy, oh, Boy . . . (*Puts broom away.*) A wife got to have a system . . . got to keep ahead of the work. I tell you, in Old Country, women had their babies in the field. And you know what they do? They pick 'em up and go right back to work without missin' a beat. What's the matter, hon? You don't look so good. You got pain? (*She puts her hand on Iris's tummy; Iris recoils slightly.*) Just a big kick, maybe, huh? That ain't nothin'. That kinda pain you soon forget. (*She pours two cups of coffee.*) Come sit with me . . . take a l'il coffee. Oh, boy . . . that was such a crazy song with the hat. Boy-oh-boy, did I laugh. Someday when old man is in a good mood, I get you to sing for him. You should hear him play accordian. Come sing it again, so I remember! You want me to get the hat? (*Iris shakes her head.*) So sing!

IRIS. (*In cracked whisper.*)
WHERE DID YOU GET THAT HAT . . .
WHERE DID YOU GET THAT TILE . . . (*She can't continue.*)

MARIE. (*Sees newspaper clipping.*) So . . . Now you know.

IRIS. What?

MARIE. Now you know . . . what you know.

IRIS. (*Pause.*) Yes.

MARIE. Are you frightened of me?

IRIS. No.

MARIE. Is that the truth?

IRIS. (*Hurries to her coat.*) No.

MARIE. Where you goin', child?

IRIS. Away.

MARIE. You don't drive.

IRIS. I'll hitchhike.

MARIE. Where? And what you gonna use for money?

IRIS. The baby's piggy bank.

MARIE. That ain't even gonna get you to Pittsburgh. (*Pause.*) Come here, honey. (*No response.*) All right . . . so don't come here. (*Beat.*) You think I'm crazy? You think maybe I'm gonna shoot you, too?

IRIS. (*Whispers.*) Nobody told me.

MARIE. Nobody didn't know how to tell you.

IRIS. Joe should have told me.

MARIE. Did *you* always did what you should?

IRIS. No . . . (*Begins to cry.*) I want to go away from here. I want to go home. (*Really breaks down.*) I want to go home . . . right now . . .

MARIE. Ohh, my . . . oi-yoi-yoi-yoi . . . come here to me. (*She moves to hold Iris. Iris backs away.*) OK . . . OK . . . Give me your hand. Come on, give to me. (*Grabs Iris's hand firmly.*) *Now*, I put your hand here. (*Puts the hand to her breast.*) Do you feel a heart? (*No response.*) Is beating? (*Iris nods.*) Then I am flesh and blood?

IRIS. Yes.

MARIE. With feelings?

IRIS. (*Barely audible.*) Yes.

MARIE. All right. Then I can put my arm around you . . . so. And the Momma give the daughter big hug . . . and the daughter give the Momma big hug . . . and we dry the tears . . . (*Marie holds Iris close.*) Someday you'll understand . . . perhaps when you are a mother yourself. Now come. (*She draws Iris toward the rocking chair.*) Sit in my lap. Don't be shy . . . that's it. You ain't too big to sit in a lap. (*Iris sits reluctantly, with embarrassment.*) Oh, boy . . there ain't nothing better than a rocking chair . . . God made them for mothers. . . . (*She rocks Iris like a baby.*) Pretty soon you'll get used to this place.

IRIS. I won't.

MARIE. You will. You big woman now. You gonna have a baby. You got to forget the things you dream as a girl.

IRIS. I'm scared.

MARIE. Of bein' a Momma?

IRIS. I won't know what to do.

MARIE. You'll know. What makes a good mother is in the heart. You don't need to learn it. It comes down the pipe with the child. Suddenly, you know from God what to do, how to be . . . like a dog you protect with your teeth if you have to. (*She sighs.*) When Kattie was born, she was black, black like coal. The midwife woulda give up on her but I grab that little body and I breathe in her myself . . . everything I had. Maybe I breathe too much. Maybe that's why she's the way she is. (*A moment. Iris suddenly winces. Her labor has begun.*)

IRIS. (*Whispering.*) Marie . . .

MARIE. What is it, Honey?

IRIS. Marie!

MARIE. Iris?

IRIS. Help me!

MARIE. My God . . . it's time. OK. OK . . . Hang on to me. There! Breathe in deep . . . deep . . . deep. That's it. Hold it. Now breathe out . . . all the way out. (*Iris screams.*) It ain't nothin', hon. Nothin' at all. This been goin' on since the world began.

IRIS. Oh, God, where's Joe? *Joe!*

MARIE. This ain't time for men. Now, sit down. An' count one . . . two . . . three . . . four, like that 'till the next pain . . . I'm gonna get the doctor. (*She exits.*)

IRIS. (*To audience.*) Doctor! That was a relief. (*Iris gets up with difficulty, walks behind screen. Only her head is visible as she changes clothes.*) With all the talk about women in Hungary giving birth in the fields, I had half a dark notion they'd carry me out to the squash patch and expect me to come back in with the baby under one arm and the squash harvest under the other. (*Hungarian lullaby begins softly on the accordian.*) But I did get to a hospital. Easy labor. No complications. (*The sound of baby crying.*) It was a lovely baby. A girl. Joe wanted to call her Josephine Dimaggio Kovacs, but I put me foot down there. (*Baby cries fade.*) Only trouble was, once the baby arrived, all my excuses departed. No more escaping the coal picking chores. Long as I was there, I had to do me bit, didn't I? Just like every other woman in Willard Patch. Up in the morning, rain or shine, over on the old slag heap. (*She emerges from the screen, unpregnant.*) Not exactly stimulating. (*Katrine enters with the infant. She kisses it and hands it to Iris, then exits.*) Where there's life, there's hope, eh? (*Holds the baby close.*) Oh, God . . . old Freda would've laughed, wouldn't she? She'd never've believed yours truly could learn how to work hard. I can just imagine what she'd have said if she'd seen that bloody, great, black mountain, all covered with little polka dots of women . . . me included . . . digging and picking and poking. She'd have thought I'd dreamed it up. She would have thought that I was stark, staring crackers. (*Wistfully.*) And now that I look back on it, I think I was. (*Blackout. Music fades under as the voice of a sportscaster giving a baseball play-by-play takes over and continues into the next scene.*)

ACT II

SCENE 2

A few weeks later. The kitchen.
It is mid-afternoon. Joe, wearing baseball cap, is seated at the
table. He is eating with one hand and rocking the baby buggy
with the other. A Pittsburgh Pirates pennant has been taped to
the side of the buggy. As the scene opens, we hear the radio play-
ing loudly. It is a Pirates game. A home run has just been hit.

JOE. And you can kiss it . . . Gooooo. . . . ooooood. . . .
BYE!!!!!!! (*He jumps up excitedly and races the buggy around the*
kitchen.) How 'bout that, l'il babycakes? How 'bout that Dick
Stuart? Bastard can't hit diddley-shit 'less he's pinch-hittin' but
when he drills one . . . he fuckin' *drills* one! (*Baby begins to cry.*
He turns radio off.) Goddamn, if I wouldna gone in the service
. . . wouldna married your Momma . . . I mighta made the
majors . . . had a great screwball. I know I woulda made the
Minors . . . (*Stephan enters. He's all dressed up with his watch and*
chain on and smoking a cigar.)
STEPHAN. (*Takes a beer from fridge.*) Yeah? So what? If it
wouldna been for your big mouth to feed, I coulda played accordian.
JOE. (*To baby.*) Say hi to Grandpap.
STEPHAN. (*Peers shyly at the baby.*) I could made money at it.
Ask Momma.
JOE. You still make good music.
STEPHAN. Aaaggghh . . . (*He pops the beer.*) Janos and his
sons comin' later . . . goin' a' McKeesport. Don't forget. We
gonna get the new father drunker'n a skunk again.
JOE. Jeezus, Daddy . . . I can't drink no more. I can't take it
like you can.
STEPHAN. (*Proudly.*) When you was born, the guys took me
to Pittsburgh. Only time a man gets to be free . . . when his ol'
lady givin' birth. (*Joe laughs.*) I didn't even see you till you was a
week old. (*They both laugh. Stephan offers a cigar, Joe shakes his*
head.) We knew how to celebrate years ago. (*He picks up his accor-*
dian and plays a few bars of a lively Hungarian tune, then stops suddenly.)
JOE. Times is changed, Daddy.

53

STEPHAN. Times ain't changed. People's changed. We used to work hard . . . drink hard. Men didn't set aroun' the kitchen baby-sittin' back then. (*The instrument fans out discordantly as he puts it down. He turns radio back on and heads upstairs with beer in hand.*) Who's winnin'? (*Hesitates, looks back at Joe.*) Us?

JOE. (*Turns radio off.*) Them. (*Stephan exits; coughing. Joe stares after him sadly. The screen door opens and Marie and Katrine trudge in with heavy buckets. Iris is half in, half out behind them. All three women wear babushkas, long canvas aprons and are covered in coal dust.*)

IRIS. (*Lugs bucket to the stove.*) Back, King, back. Down, sweetheart. Good daggie. . . . (*She enters, lugging bucket to the stove.*) Oooohhh. . . . I feel like a blinkin' coal miner.

KATRINE. (*Accusing.*) You only picked half a bucket.

IRIS. Well, I like that. Who dug all the bloody holes?

JOE. Company man sees you up on that slag heap, you'll all end up in jail.

IRIS. Oh, good . . . a vacation.

MARIE. (*Turns radio off.*) How you think we gonna keep the stove goin' in winter?

JOE. Winter's over.

MARIE. One winter goes . . . another comes, son. If you don't *do* today, you ain't *got* tomorrow.

JOE. Why don't you sit down, Momma. You look all in. From now on me 'n' Daddy'll get the coal.

MARIE. If you get coal like you paint the house — we'll all freeze to death.

JOE. You know Janos couldn't get the loan for his septic tank. You know I'm lookin' for sump'n every day . . . an' sneakin' off to Welfare . . . so Daddy don't know. (*Lowers his voice.*) I gotta go there right now.

IRIS. (*Firmly.*) Well, I'm coming with you this time.

JOE. Oh, no you ain't.

IRIS. Oh, yes, I am. I'm getting out of this house today . . . like it or lump it, Joe Kovacs.

JOE. I ain't havin' my wife watch me beg for money.

KATRINE. She's startin' trouble, Momma.

IRIS. Any beggin' to be done, Duckie, we'll do it together . . . and I want to stop at Woolworth's on the way home. (*She begins to undress.*)

JOE. Don't tell *me* what we're gonna do!

MARIE. Daddy's got a few shots in him, Joe. He's playin' music. He ain't gonna see. Take your wife.

JOE. It don't have nothin' to do with him. I said she ain't goin'—and she ain't.

IRIS. Try and stop me.

JOE. I don't have to. I'll just get in the car and drive off.

IRIS. I'll throw meself under the wheels.

JOE. Then I'll drive over you.

IRIS. (*Cheerfully.*) Good. And if I'm still alive, I'll drag me broken body, covered with tire tracks, up to the pike and hitch-hike.

JOE. (*Softening.*) Hey . . . You been hittin' on Daddy's vodka, kid?

IRIS. (*Jumps on the chair.*) No. I just stood up on the slag heap this morning and I said to meself: Iris, old girl, the time has come to get off the plantation. Today's the day, I said. Woolworth's or bust!

JOE. You're nuts!

IRIS. C'mon, Joe, what do you say?

MARIE. Take her, son.

JOE. (*Long pause.*) Agh . . . go get cleaned up.

IRIS. (*Jumping down.*) Hurray! (*Runs up to bedroom.*) Joe?

JOE. What?

IRIS. I love you.

JOE. I better never catch you hitchhikin', woman!

IRIS. Only if I have to. (*She disappears.*)

JOE. (*He listens to her singing.*) You s'pposed to be straightenin' her out . . . not stirrin' her up.

MARIE. (*Urgently.*) Don't be so tough. Forget the paint. Forget the coal. We been pickin' all these years, we can go on pickin'. And forget Daddy. You look for work outa state. One man outa work is bad enough—two men out don't make no sense.

STEPHAN. (*Entering. Dressed for hunting now.*) What's goin' on? What are ya? A woman? You stand gossiping?

JOE. I was just tellin' Momma, pickin' on the heap is trouble. Them company men's armed. I was sayin' *I* should do it.

STEPHAN. Damn right! (*He slaps Marie's behind good-naturedly.*) You gettin' too long in the tooth for pickin', old woman. I go with you, Son. Tomorrow, OK? (*He gets gun.*)

JOE. Goin' huntin'?

55

STEPHAN. I want Janos to take a look at the bolt. She don't slide good. Gettin' old and tired like me.

JOE. What kinda talk is that, Daddy?

STEPHAN. Spit my damn tooth out this mornin'.

JOE. That ain't 'cause you're gettin' old and tired . . . that's cause you walked into Wiggin's fist outside Sneaky's last night.

STEPHAN. Goddam sumbitch scab . . .

MARIE. That was years ago.

STEPHAN. Once a scab, always a scab . . . Comin' beer garden for 'n hour?

JOE. I can't.

STEPHAN. I ain't so broke I can't buy my only son a beer.

JOE. I know that, Daddy. I gotta go someplace. (*Iris appears at the top of the stairs in the red birthday dress. Although it is still very long, Marie has altered it so that it fits nicely now. Iris's hair is down and she wears vivid lipstick. Marie tries in vain to signal her back.*)

IRIS. Ta-dah! (*Turns so Joe can see dress.*) Ohh . . .

STEPHAN. (*Quietly.*) That where you goin', Joe? Show your wife's legs around Daisyville?

JOE. Don't talk like that.

STEPHAN. Gonna show that Johnny Bull off to the Hunky rapers?

IRIS. Joe is going to take me for a ride, Mr. Kovacs.

MARIE. She ain't been nowhere, since she got here, Stephan.

STEPHAN. Get outa that whore dress.

IRIS. I beg your pardon.

JOE. Shut up, Iris.

IRIS: I won't shut up. I have no intention of taking off this dress.

STEPHAN. This is *my* house!

MARIE. Istvan . . .

JOE. Go change, Iris.

STEPHAN. An' wipe that damn lipstick off, while you're at it.

IRIS. No.

STEPHAN. I give you five, Johnny Bull!

IRIS. I am nineteen years old.

STEPHAN. One . . .

IRIS. I have a right to live my own life.

STEPHAN. Two . . .

IRIS. And don't call me a Johnny Bull anymore . . .

STEPHAN. Three . . .

JOE. You stupid bitch, you can't go decked out like that to the Welfare, any damn way . . . (*Joe realizes his mistake. There is a long dangerous pause.*)

STEPHAN. (*Softly.*) Who's goin' to Welfare?

JOE. *I* am.

STEPHAN. (*Contemptuously.*) Welfare! (*He spits on the floor.*)

JOE. That's right.

STEPHAN. You nothin' but a damn pussy now. Ain't been worth a *shit* since you come back from England! (*Katrine moves mechanically to wipe up the spit.*)

JOE. I'll get it. (*Joe stoops at his father's feet to clean up the spit with his handkerchief.*) Now get outa here, Kattie! Out!

STEPHAN. And the same goes for you! Out! Out with your damn Welfare! No one in my house is gonna stoop that low.

IRIS. Yes, he does have to stoop that low, Mr. Kovacs — like a lot of other men around here — It's not Joe's fault there's no work.

MARIE. The town gives him twenty dollars a week and all the streets he can sweep.

JOE. (*Standing suddenly.*) And plenty more guys sweepin' the same damn street I just swept.

STEPHAN. Any bum gets a handout in this country, he better bust ass.

JOE. That what I am, a bum?

STEPHAN. You takin' that kind money, you a bum.

IRIS. No. You are a demobilized United States soldier. (*To Stephan.*) He *deserves* help till he gets a job.

STEPHAN. Red for whore. Red for Communist.

MARIE. Oi-yoi-yoi . . . (*She picks up the baby.*)

IRIS. Don't you dare call me . . .

JOE. Get in that bedroom, Iris, an' get into somethin' you can ride the car in. *Move!* (*Iris runs into the bedroom.*)

JOE. Now, if you don't mind, sir. I'd like to get goin', do what I have to do.

STEPHAN. Go right ahead. Get into the Buick and head out West to your sumbitch brother. You both the same damn thing. I don't need either one a' younse.

JOE. What I'm gonna do is get in that Buick with my wife and drive down to Town Hall and sign for my check. Then I'm gonna take Iris to see my high school . . . an' maybe take her to Woolworth's, get some l'il jingle-dangle for the baby . . . like normal people . . . and from now on that's what we're gonna be is normal.

STEPHAN. Bums.

JOE. I'd sooner be that, than sittin' up Sneaky Pete's sayin' how fine an' dandy Eisenhower is. Every damn one of younse fightin', cussin', shootin' each other's toes off an' puttin' bullet holes in Sneaky's ceilin'. Yellin' 'bout Russia this 'n' that . . . nigger's this an' that . . . steada the real problem. How many a you had your heads stove in by strikebreakers, one after another ass thrown in jail, families half-starved an' robbed a your money? And still there ain't one a younse know who the hell did it to you . . . or why!

STEPHAN. An' you do?

JOE. All I know is you been screwed. Alla you. Screwed by the bosses, fucked over by the government, and left behind by a union gone crooked.

STEPHAN. You learn that red talk in England.

JOE. I didn't learn it nowhere but what I been hearin' ever since I been back.

STEPHAN. This is the best goddamn country in the world.

JOE. Chicken in every pot.

STEPHAN. Few years down the mine teach you a lesson.

JOE. There ain't no goddamn mine no more. And there ain't *gonna* be no more mine.

STEPHAN. Things will open up again and then I show you how a *real* man works.

JOE. In a pig's eye they'll open up . . . and even if they did, nobody ain't gonna put you back to work. You're too old, Daddy! *You're too damn old! Understand? (Iris appears from the bedroom in her housedress and babushka.)*

STEPHAN. *(After a long, painful pause, he says to Marie what he cannot bring himself to say to his son.)* If Janos fix this gun, Marie . . .

JOE. I'm sorry, Daddy . . .

STEPHAN. If Janos fix, then I go huntin' tonight.

JOE. Don't go jackin' deer with headlights.

STEPHAN. You gonna have plenty food, Marie.

MARIE. We always had what to eat from you, Stephan.

STEPHAN. And when there was work, did I work?

MARIE. All your life.

STEPHAN. An' how old I was when I begin work?

MARIE. Nine years old.

STEPHAN. An' what did they pay me, Momma? Nine years old, down the mine, up to my chin in freezin' water, holes where even the mules wouldn't go, fourteen hours straight!

MARIE. Fifty cents a day . . .

STEPHAN. Forty-five cents for my mother . . . a nickel for me . . . an' a pack a Camels. (*His voice rises bitterly.*) Don't forget the goddamn Camels! I don't want my son to think there wasn't no benefits. (*He strides to the door.*) I was born workin' . . . I'll drop dead workin'! (*He slams out.*)

MARIE. Don't fret, Joe. It had to be said. He'll get over it.

JOE. He won't get over it. (*Marie exits with the baby.*) Get Iris a jacket, Kattie. It's gonna get cold. (*Katrine exits.*)

JOE. I'm sorry you had to hear that.

IRIS. It's all right. You stood up for yourself, Joe.

JOE. Stood up for what? I ain't never spoke to my father that way before. Aghh, *shit!* I can't please nobody! (*He yells.*) Kattie! Hurry up with that goddamn jacket! (*To Iris.*) 'Cause I'm takin' my wife to the city . . . show her them big, fine, fancy houses with the statues in the yard . . . so she can really she what she's missin'.

KATRINE. (*Entering.*) She ain't goin' nowhere. Daddy took the Buick. (*Joe kicks a chair.*)

IRIS. Don't get upset, Joe.

JOE. What the hell'm I s'posed to do don't get upset? Jeezus fuckin' H. Christ! (*Desperately.*) I *need* my car. Them're *my* wheels! I worked nights . . . three fuckin' years for that Buick. He ran it to hell . . . (*Close to tears.*) Back n' forth . . . back n' forth to that goddamn coal mine . . . in that red-dog filth . . . that sulpher sludge. That car used to be pink . . . baby pink.

IRIS. C'mon, Joe . . . we'll hitchhike. (*Beat.*) Let's go out that door together, lovie . . . down to the town hall and sign for our check. That's all that matters now.

JOE. (*Impossibly torn between his father's and Iris's expectations.*) Lemme tell you what matters. What matters is your mouth. You started this whole damn thing! OK! You wanna be a guy? I'll teach you how to be a guy. (*He throws open refrigerator, takes out*

59

six-pack and tosses it to Iris.) Here . . . down a couple a these babies. Kattie, set my buddy here up some tin cans. Bring that Winchester. Won't nobody accuse her ever again a' bein' a girl when I get through with her! (*He slams out. Katrine gets gun, takes beer from Iris and follows her brother out.*)

IRIS. (*To audience with rueful smile, as she dons an apron.*) Made me drink three bottles of that stuff. American beer with bubbles. I got a terrible headache. (*She washes her hands, removes the towel from rising bread dough and takes pans from the stove. As she continues to speak to the audience, she shapes the rolls and loaves, greasing each pan efficiently before placing the dough in.*) Watching cowboy movies, you'd think there's only one end of a gun could cause damage, wouldn't you? Not true. (*Gun shot is heard.*) By the finish of that afternoon, I thought I'd have to have me right shoulder amputated. And I never hit one of those targets . . . (*Couple more shots are heard.*) Though I did nick a couple of chimneys I wasn't aiming at. (*Another shot.*) So I wasn't sorry when he stamped off, cursing, down the road. (*Marie enters with laundry basket and ironing board. Katrine follows with the baby. They are unaware of Iris as they go about their chores.*) Never thought I'd say this, but I felt quite relieved to get back to the women and the bread dough. (*Seriously.*) Still, you know, one thing had dawned on me. If Joe was ever going to pack our bags, that would've been the day he'd have done it. (*Wipes her hands.*) But he didn't. (*The baby begins whimpering, softly at first. Iris hurries to her infant and takes her from Katrine. Cooing gently, the young mother exits. The baby cries grow more insistent off stage. Marie goes to the table, stares at the bread, then in the direction of the noise. The lights fade quickly to black. The sounds of infant distress grow louder and continue to the beginning of the next scene.*)

ACT II
SCENE 3

Early evening of the same day. The lights come up in the kitchen. Katrine is lighting the kerosene lamp. Marie is putting the rolls in the oven. There are two piles of neatly ironed clothing on the ironing board. Iris enters with a sketch pad. She moves the piles of laundry and prepares to use the ironing board as a place to draw.

MARIE. Don't be mad at Daddy.

IRIS. I'll get back to the ironing later.

MARIE. You done enough, honey.

IRIS. I promised you a drawing of yourself with your bread.

MARIE. Daddy got too much pride . . . (*She sits in the rocker with a breadloaf.*) He don't mean half what he say.

IRIS. (*Gently.*) It's all right, Marie. Don't worry yourself. (*She begins to sketch.*)

MARIE. You don't draw flowers no more.

IRIS. If I'm going to be a real artist, I've got to learn how to draw people, haven't I?

MARIE. Don't make me too fancy. Nobody won't know it's me.

IRIS. I'm trying to make you look the way you are.

MARIE. What way is that?

IRIS. Like Marie.

MARIE. (*Sadly.*) Marie , . . who is Marie? There's Marie the coal picker . . . Marie the mother . . . Marie the wife . . . (*Pause.*) Marie the murderer . . .

IRIS. Don't let's talk about it today.

MARIE. I'm sorry to tell you over and over . . . make you crazy, hon.

IRIS. I . . . I . . . want to talk to you about . . .

MARIE. You the only one I ever had to tell my story to.

IRIS. I know, duck. But I . . .

MARIE. Daddy don't want to hear. Joe don't say nothin' . . .

IRIS. Marie, please listen to . . .

MARIE. You see them women up on the slag heap? Sure they say, "Hi, Marie. How you doin', Marie?" . . . but I know how they talk. "Look," they say, "She killed a man and now she's runnin' around free." (*A teardrop escapes.*) Free?

IRIS. Don't cry, Marie.

MARIE. Go watch TV, Kattie. *Move!* (*Katrine exits reluctantly.*)

IRIS. (*Tenderly.*) Look . . . would you like me to tell you a joke? You like jokes.

MARIE. Oi-yoi-yoi-yoi . . . I cried for two years after I did that.

IRIS. I've got a new joke for you.

MARIE. No one else weep . . . only me.

IRIS. P'raps you did the crying for everyone else.

MARIE. Yeah. Some time I felt I was cryin' for the whole world. But . . . everything pass. No? One day I got up and all the tears had dried. But I ain't free, Iris. I gotta see that gun every day . . . Kattie every day. Even now I don't know who I kill that man for. For Kattie? For myself? So some other poor girl wouldn't get it? Maybe I just couldn't take that dinner bucket bangin' on the swing.

IRIS. I might do the same if it happened to my baby. I mean, Kattie's your baby, isn't she?

MARIE. When everyone is gone, she'll be my company. You know, no matter how much I slap that big cow, when I sit little bit at night, watch TV, she put her head in my lap and her thumb in that big mouth that drive me so crazy . . . and I feel a big love . . . (*She gets up wearily.*) Oi-yoi . . . you can cut the cord to the mother's belly but not to the heart. (*Crosses to Iris to look at the sketch.*) You better stick to shoes and flowers. I don't look that good.

IRIS. You've got a lovely face.

MARIE. I'm old and ugly.

IRIS. You're not! Your face shows how you feel. When you feel "Oi-yoi-yoi", then you look "Oi-yoi-yoi." When you feel "Boy-oh-boy" then you look blinkin' marvellous, don't you?

MARIE. (*Laughs.*) You got l'il bit Hungarian blood, I think . . . so wise you're becoming.

IRIS. Feel a bit better?

MARIE. Sure.

IRIS. Enough for me to talk to you? (*The baby gurgles. Marie hurries to the buggy — an effort to avoid the words Iris is trying to say.*)

MARIE. Uhh-oh! Somebody's awake! (*She picks up the baby.*) Ohhh, come to Bubba. Oh, what a pretty, pretty. Your Grandpap been sulkin' 'cause you don't have l'il rinky-tinky-dinky between the legs. Quick with the titty, Iris. She's gettin' mad.

IRIS. I've got to keep her on her schedule.

MARIE. Oy, this new world. *I* don't like it . . . an' *she* don't like it.

IRIS. I'll put some honey on her pacifier. She likes that. (*While Iris is turned away, Marie sits in the rocker and puts her breast in the baby's mouth.*)

MARIE. There . . .

IRIS. (*Horrified.*) Marie! *What are you doing?*

MARIE. Better'n a hunk a rubber, ain't it?

IRIS. You can't do that!

MARIE. This is the way the grandmother do in Old Country.

IRIS. Not in *my* Old Country!

MARIE. Aghhh . . this ol' titty is still good.

IRIS. That's not the point.

MARIE. Look, we do half your way, new way . . . an' half old way, *my* way.

IRIS. Oh, no.

MARIE. Come sit.

IRIS. I can't sit in front of you and watch you do that.

MARIE. So sit behind me. (*Iris reluctantly draws up a chair, sits back to back with Marie,* D.C., *in profile to the audience.*) Now tell me the joke.

IRIS. (*Slightly annoyed.*) What joke?

MARIE. You said you gotta new joke.

IRIS. I forget it now.

MARIE. So tell me an old one. Tell me the one about the queen's mamma again. C'mon!

IRIS. (*Reluctantly at first.*) Well . . . see, the queen's mum went to see this big opera in London and half way through she had to go and pee. . .

MARIE. You never think a them queens havin' to pee.

IRIS. So . . . she goes down to the ladies room . . . (*Begins to enter into the spirit.*) But can't find the fancy one meant for royalty, so she pops in the loo the usherettes use . . . And there's these two stalls, see . . .

MARIE. An' there ain't no paper in the john where the queen's mamma is . . .

IRIS. Right . . . so the queen's mum sees these two little feet next door . . .

MARIE. So she knock . . . (*Rapping on the arm of the rocker.*)

IRIS. And says: (*Upper-class accent.*) "I say have you any paper on your side?"

MARIE. Oh, boy-oh-boy . . . I love this joke.

IRIS. And this usherette's voice says back: (*Cockney.*) "No, sorry, love!" So the queen mum sits a bit longer, knocks again: (*Marie raps on the chair.*) "I say, do you have a hanky in your bag?" So the usherette shouts back: "Not a bloody thing, duckie!"

63

MARIE. So then the queen's mamma knock the third time, no?
IRIS. Knocks again, yes. (*Marie raps.*) And says: "I say . . . do you happen to have two fivers for a ten?"
MARIE. (*Laughing heartily.*) Oh, boy-oh-boy-oh-boy . . . I'm gonna tell that one to the man at the store . . . Oh, boy, is it good. (*Still chuckling she puts her breast away.*) You can look now, Iris. Titty's gone. Baby sound asleep. (*Somewhere the sound of an accordian playing a lively czardas begins.*) Listen, someone playin' . . . not as good as Daddy . . . but nice, huh? (*She puts the baby down.*) Come on, Iris . . . I show you Hungarian good time. We dance! (*The music grows more insistent.*)
IRIS. But Marie, you said . . .
MARIE. We talk all you want tomorrow. OK? Now, I'm gonna show you the czardas! You think Hunkies don't know how to have fun? (*Spins Iris around.*) This is the way *my* people enjoy when they are happy. That's it! You know how . . . Oh, I ain't done this for years! (*Kicks the chairs out of the way.*) One, two, three . . .
IRIS. And one, two, three . . .
MARIE. What you want for dinner tonight? Goulash?
IRIS. Pig's feet!
MARIE. Pig's feet you got! (*They whirl around the kitchen and dance offstage. Lights fade to the sound of their laughter.*)

ACT II

Scene 4

Very late the same night. The kitchen. Katrine in nightgown is alone filling the kerosene lamp. Suddenly, the outside door bangs open. Stephan stands swaying, very drunk. His hands and clothes are blood-stained from gutting a deer.

STEPHAN. Where's your Momma?
KATRINE. Upstairs.
STEPHAN. An' the Johnny Bull?
KATRINE. Sleepin'.
STEPHAN. Well, you go tell them, they got what to eat for next week. Nobody goes hungry in this house . . . not while

Stephan Kovacs is alive.

KATRINE. You gotta deer, Daddy?

STEPHAN. 'S hangin' onna porch.

KATRINE. Game warden see ya?

STEPHAN. Game warden can go fuck himself. (*He takes a beer from the fridge.*) Get a bucket under that doe! I don't want your mother scrubbin' blood all day tomorrow.

KATRINE. I gotta do this. Momma said.

STEPHAN. (*Grabs kerosene from her.*) *Move!* Take that bucket out! (*Katrine goes out with bucket. Still holding the kerosene, Stephan drinks thirstily. Katrine's face appears outside the door screen.*) You put bucket?

KATRINE. Yeah . . . Daddy?

STEPHAN. Now get to bed.

KATRINE. There's somebody in the squash patch.

STEPHAN. Sumadambitch! Get in here! (*Goes to door.*)

KATRINE. I seen a match light. Back there. See?

STEPHAN. I don't need to see . . . I know who the hell it is. He wanna light a match, I'll light him a match. (*Katrine enters. She's in his way. He pushes her aside and lurches out with the gun and kerosene.*)

KATRINE. *Momma!* (*Marie enters in nightgown and robe.*)

MARIE. I hear, I hear. What's goin' on?

KATRINE. Daddy's drunk. He pushed me, Momma.

MARIE. He's mad today, honey. He don't mean it.

KATRINE. I was fillin' the lamp, like you tol' me.

MARIE. You good girl.

KATRINE. Daddy got a deer.

IRIS. (*Entering in nightgown.*) Poor thing.

MARIE. You're eatin' deer meat, Iris. It don't come from no supermarket. (*To Katrine.*) You put bucket under? (*Katrine nods.*) Where'd Daddy go?

KATRINE. There was somebody in the squash. He went after 'em.

MARIE. (*Hurries to the door with Iris.*) Stephan! You come in here! (*Marie returns.*) Old fool. Who was it? Why you didn't put this cap back on the kerosene?

KATRINE. Daddy took it.

MARIE. You sure?

KATRINE. Had it in his hand.

MARIE. Why?

IRIS. Marie. Look, a fire! Look!

MARIE. Mother of God . . . (*She grabs her coat, runs to the door.*)
Kattie, fill couple buckets a water. Quick! Iris call Elvira-Mae
for fire truck! (*Throws coat on.*) I knew it would come to this . . .
(*There's a few moments of frantic activity among the women. Iris tries
dialing. Suddenly Stephan enters, gun in hand.*)

STEPHAN. Kattie! Get me six-pack a beer! Marie, gimmee
couple pillows for the back swing! That sumbitch Wiggins
been stealin' me blind for years . . . an' now I'm gonna watch
his ass fry! Find me pack a' Camels, Marie! Hurry!

IRIS. Hello? Elvira-Mae?

STEPHAN. What the hell you think you're doin', Johnny Bull?

MARIE. Istvan, *I* told her to call.

STEPHAN. Get away from my phone!

IRIS. It's *my* phone. Hello? Hello? Elvira . . .

STEPHAN. (*Grabs the receiver.*) Everythin' outside that door
belong to somebody else. (*He hangs up.*) Everthin' inside the
door belong to me.

IRIS. Then I better put myself *outside* the door, hadn't I?

STEPHAN. Sooner the better.

MARIE. There might be somebody in that house!

STEPHAN. Strikebreakers!

MARIE. Human bein's!

STEPHAN. Scabs! You stood against them yourself . . . on the
picket line, with a shovel in your hand!

MARIE. Didn't stop me feelin' sorry that the poor was fightin'
the poor. (*She heads to door with a bucket of water.*)

STEPHAN. (*Frustrated, shouting.*) What do women know how a
man feels when he can't take care of his own?

MARIE. You think I don't know? Wiggins' wife know, too.
(*Stephan slaps her.*)

IRIS. Stop it!

MARIE. Neighbor turned against neighbor . . . that's the real
shame.

STEPHAN. When a neighbor abuse your daughter, did you
shake his hand? (*Pause.*) Now go get my fuckin' pillows.

JOE. (*Entering from outside.*) What's goin' on here?

MARIE. (*Deeply upset.*) Ask your father . . . I don't care if the whole damn patch burns to the ground . . . an' me with it! (*She slams outside.*)

JOE. You set that fire over Wiggins, Daddy?

STEPHAN. Last time that bastard step foot in *my* yard.

JOE. He wasn't in your damn yard. *I* was. That was *me* out there! (*While Stephan is distracted by Joe, Iris dives for the phone again. Suddenly, the old man levels his gun at her. Whispers.*) Daddy, no . . .

STEPHAN. I told you leave my phone be. (*Iris is frozen with fear.*)

JOE. Daddy, gimme the gun . . .

STEPHAN. She been askin' for it. Now she got it.

JOE. Easy . . . easy now . . .

IRIS. (*Barely audible.*) Joe . . . he's going to shoot me . . .

JOE. Be quiet an' drop the phone, Iris. Drop it! (*The receiver falls.*) See, Daddy, she let it go. C'mon now . . . lemme have the gun . . . easy . . . C'mon . . . we'll take a walk . . . just you an' me . . . (*Stephan releases the safety catch.*)

IRIS. Please . . .

STEPHAN. Just who in the *hell* do you think you are? *Who?*

IRIS. (*A whisper.*) I don't know.

JOE. She's my wife, Daddy . . . an' the mother a that baby over there.

STEPHAN. An' does she say what goes on here? Or *me?*

JOE. You're the boss. You know that.

STEPHAN. Don't lie to me! (*He swings the gun in Joe's direction.*) She's gonna make you run from us with your goddamn tail between your snivelin' legs . . .

JOE. She ain't makin' me do nothin'. I'm my own man. (*Great emotion.*) Goddamn it, Daddy . . . I'm trying to be my own man.

STEPHAN. Just like your brother.

JOE. He left. I didn't.

STEPHAN. Just like Pishta.

JOE. I ain't walkin' out on my family like he did. I ain't leavin' none a' younse behind. All's I thought about in England was comin' home here an' . . .

STEPHAN. You didn't think about nothin' but *her!* (*He turns the*

gun back on Iris.) Well, maybe she's runnin' you . . . but she ain't
. . .

MARIE. (*Entering.*) You crazy, old fool!

STEPHAN. Stay back!

MARIE. Shame on you! (*She places herself between Iris and the gun and wrenches it fiercely from his hands.*) You who could not kill Krutchik . . . now you gonna point the gun at your own daughter-in-law? Ain't there been enough killin' in this house?

JOE. Shut up, Momma.

IRIS. I know about it, Joe.

MARIE. She knowed a long time what I done. (*Calmly but with authority.*) Now take the gun, Iris. Nobody won't point it at you again — not while I'm livin'. Go on! I told you long time ago I wasn't gonna baby you. So take it! I don't want you runnin' round rest of your life scared of these damn things. (*Iris takes the gun.*) That's right! Just like it was a broom. Put it in the closet. Long as we got men, we got to live with guns.

STEPHAN. (*Erupts violently.*) Get her outa my sight! (*Slams his fist on the table, the baby begins to cry.*) *I want her out from under my roof right now!*

IRIS. I'll go! Just let me get my baby!

STEPHAN. Oh, no . . . You ain't takin' my grandchild with you. (*He lurches towards the buggy.*) You go out the way you came in, Johnny Bull, *with nothin'.*

IRIS. (*Raises the gun instinctively.*) Leave that baby alone!

JOE. Iris! What're you doin'?

IRIS. Get away! Everybody just get away from me! (*She waves the gun wildly.*) Wheel that buggy in the living room!

MARIE. (*Hurriedly following orders.*) I got her, Iris. Don't worry. Give the gun to Joe. (*She returns immediately and closes the door.*)

IRIS. I mean it! Move back, Joe! And you, Stephan! (*They step back.*) Now sit down!

MARIE. C'mon . . . one crazy is enough!

JOE. You're gonna hurt somebody.

IRIS. And it might be you so shut up! (*Stephan slumps into a chair with low moan and covers his face with his hands. Joe sits too.*)

JOE. So we're sittin'.

IRIS. Now, Kattie, you get over there and phone!

JOE. For Chrissakes . . .

IRIS. Pick up that phone, Kattie!

KATRINE. (*Gets up from the corner where she has been watching the proceedings with interest. She takes her thumb from her mouth.*) I don't know how!

IRIS. *Then learn!*

KATRINE. No!

IRIS. *Move!* (*Katrine obeys.*) Now put your finger in that last hole with the zero . . . now turn it all the way around . . . *all the way around!* Now let it go! Take your bloody finger out of the hole! Right!

JOE. You're bein' an asshole.

KATRINE. She's askin' . . .

IRIS. Tell her there's a fire in Willard Patch.

JOE. Iris, *I been over there.* All's he got was a couple a tomato bushes an' a piece a the damn porch. I put it out with my jacket.

IRIS. Well, we'll just make sure, won't we? Kattie, tell Elvira to call the fire department.

KATRINE. Iris said send fire truck to Willard.

IRIS. Tell her Wiggins' house.

KATRINE. Wiggins' house.

IRIS. Say *quick!*

KATRINE. Quick!

IRIS. Now hang up! (*Katrine obeys.*) You did a good job, Kattie.

JOE. I oughta whip your ass.

MARIE. Leave her be.

IRIS. (*Puts gun away.*) Just like a broom, Marie . . . back in the closet . . . 'til tomorrow.

JOE. Now get to bed!

IRIS. No. I'm going out that door, Joe.

JOE. Be a cold day in hell!

IRIS. Your father's made himself quite clear.

JOE. My father's drunk.

IRIS. He's never wanted me here.

JOE. He would if you'd keep your mouth shut! Take a look at the poor bastard. You think he knows what the hell he's sayin'?

IRIS. I'm leaving. You can come or not come, Joe. It's up to you.

KATRINE. You goin' to California . . . see Pishta, Iris?

JOE. She ain't goin' nowhere!

IRIS. Please come with me, Joe.

STEPHAN. (*Moans.*) Pishta . . .

MARIE. Oi-yoi-yoi-yoi. . . . (*She moves quickly to her husband.*)

STEPHAN. (*Deeply upset.*) Ohhh, my God . . . Pishta . . . Pishta . . .

MARIE. What's the matter, Istvan?

STEPHAN. Why'd he go away? Why? I woulda give him every damn thing I had . . . Pishta . . .

MARIE. You did the best you could . . . you ain't God.

STEPHAN. If I'da shot Krutchik, you wouldn't had to done it, Marie. That's the last words Pishta said to me.

MARIE. It's past, Istvan. (*She holds him as he weeps.*) Take him, Joe. Stay with him.

JOE. C'mon Daddy . . . C'mon . . . I'll take you a walk . . . down the coke ovens . . . talk a l'il . . .

STEPHAN. I don't want nobody to go away.

JOE. (*He stares at Iris.*) Nobody's goin'.

STEPHAN. She can stay . . . your wife can stay, Joe.

JOE. She knows that.

STEPHAN. Momma wants her to stay.

JOE. She'll stay. She'll stay.

STEPHAN. I'm so damn sorry.

JOE. It's OK . . . (*Joe helps Stephan to his feet.*) C'mon . . . c'mon now . . .

STEPHAN. This is the best goddamn country in the world, ain't it, Joe?

JOE. Yes, sir! (*They go outside.*)

STEPHAN'S VOICE. Things'll open up again, son.

JOE'S VOICE. We'll take a ride up Union Hall tomorrow . . . see what's doin'. (*The baby begins to whimper softly. Iris goes into the living room to get her.*)

MARIE. I've seen this before. Coupla days he'll be OK.

IRIS. (*Re-entering.*) I'm sorry.

MARIE. Everybody's sorry . . me, Daddy, Joe . . . now you. (*She sits in the rocking chair.*) Come sit beside me. (*Iris kneels with the Baby. Marie strokes Iris' hair.*) No more little innocent Johnny Bull, eh?

IRIS. No. (*Katrine kneels on the other side of Marie, puts her head on her mother's lap with her thumb in her mouth.*)

MARIE. He's a good man Daddy. So he drink a l'il bit.

IRIS. I s'pose I would, too, if I were him.

MARIE. He got to wash that coal dust outa his throat. He don't mean what he say about you. He don't mean what he say about the colored. He just feels so low himself, he got to make somebody else lower. But he ain't so bad . . . (*The lights begin to fade on Marie, Katrine, Iris and the baby, three generations, forming a visual triangle with Marie at the apex. A gentle melody from a neighbor's accordian takes over.*)

KATRINE. If you go to California, Iris . . . see Pishta . . . can I go with you?

IRIS. I won't be going to California, Kattie. I don't suppose it's all roses there, either. (*Pause.*) Nothing ever is, is it? (*Lights fade out leaving a spotlight on the four females.*)

MARIE. You hear accordian . . . how nice. Daddy coulda made money at that if things had been different. (*Black out. A fire truck screams by and fades.*)

ACT II

Scene 5

The next night. In the black, we hear Katrine calling Iris softly. Each time we hear Iris's name, it is accompanied by the sound of a doorknob rattling. This can be a tape recording if necessary.

IRIS'S VOICE. Kattie?

KATRINE'S VOICE. It ain't Santie Claus.

IRIS'S VOICE. What are you doing up so late?

KATRINE'S VOICE. After what you done last night . . . actin crazy . . . Joe says I gotta watch younse.

IRIS'S VOICE. I don't like being watched.

KATRINE'S VOICE. I know . . . but he gimme a dollar. (*The lights come up on Iris hurriedly locking her suitcase in the bedroom. She is wearing the clothes she arrived in, but her skirt hem is at a respectable length now and the shoes are more sensible. Katrine rattles the locked door again. Iris quickly puts a long robe over her street clothes, puts the suitcase near the door and throws a towel over it.*)

71

IRIS. Is Joe still up at Sneaky Pete's with your Dad? (*She opens the door.*)

KATRINE. (*In pajamas.*) Unh-huh. They watchin' the night game with Janos an' the guys. (*Entering, looks around.*) You ain't cleaned too good.

IRIS. But better now than when I came, right?

KATRINE. I clean *real* good.

IRIS. (*Fondly.*) You work very hard, Kattie.

KATRINE. I'm s'posed to stay busy. It's good for me. (*Sitting on the bed.*) You sleep OK in this?

IRIS. Yes. How would you like to sleep there? Joe'll be gone half the night. He'll fall asleep on the couch.

KATRINE. He'll whip my ass, I sleep in his bed.

IRIS. It's *your* bed.

KATRINE. I was born in it.

IRIS. That's right. (*She helps Katrine into her bed.*)

KATRINE. I like to see Joe's face, he sees this big cow under the quilt.

IRIS. How is it?

KATRINE. (*Snuggling down.*) Oh, boy . . . I like my bed. I ain't slep' right in that other'n. (*She puts her thumb in her mouth and closes her eyes. Iris tucks her in.*) Iris . . . where *you* gonna sleep?

IRIS. Ohh, I think I'll be staying up for a while.

KATRINE. Iris . . you like Joe?

IRIS. Yes. (*Close to tears.*) Do you?

KATRINE. He's my brother, ain't he? (*Iris nods.*) An' you my sister . . . *in law,* I mean.

IRIS. Yes. Yes, I am.

KATRINE. Iris . . . sump'n younse didn't notice . . . (*She holds out her arm, revealing the bracelet Iris brought her from England.*) Lucky charm bracelet.

IRIS. Ohh, Kattie . . . that's very nice . . . (*Kisses Katrine's cheek tenderly.*) Goodnight, Dear. (*She turns off the light, picks up the towel-covered suitcase and opens the door.*) Sleep tight.

KATRINE. Don't let no bedbugs bite. (*Iris closes the door and hurries down into the kitchen. She checks the baby in the buggy and then goes to the phone and dials.*)

IRIS. (*Low voice.*) Hello . . . Elvira-Mae? Yes . . . Iris again . . . no, I haven't changed my mind . . . half an hour, then? I'll be out by the gate. Thanks. (*As Iris hangs up, Marie enters from outside in her nightgown. She pretends not to see the suitcase.*)

MARIE. Cold out there . . . (*Rubbing her hands briskly.*) Oi-yoi-yoi-yoi-yoi . . . everybody up all night last night. Go to bed early tonight. Get some rest, child. You can't figure things when you're sad an' tired. (*She checks the baby.*)

IRIS. I can't stay.

MARIE. We gonna find that matchbook tomorrow, honey, an' send in for the free lessons. OK?

IRIS. I'm all packed, Marie.

MARIE. You think that Freda would believe how you can work now? How you can make bread, change diaper . . . all at the same time?

IRIS. I couldn't have done it without you . . . (*Urgently.*) But even if I learned *every single thing* you know . . . even if everybody got up laughing and singing tomorrow, and Joe got a job . . . and all the coal mines in Pennsylvania opened up again, I wouldn't be happy here. (*Voice rising in frustration.*) Don't you understand?

MARIE. Understand? (*Passionately.*) You think I never say to myself, when I work in New York, "Keep on goin', Marie. You don't have to go back there to that goddamn coal dust!" Lotta people wanted to teach me how to *do*, how to *look*, how to *read*!

IRIS. I stayed as long as I could.

MARIE. Oh, Iris . . . there's *good* people here.

IRIS. Yes.

MARIE. Good as any place. They break their backs rippin' coal from the earth so that others can sit aroun' in comfort. Did you know that?

IRIS. Yes.

MARIE. Daddy need a good wife . . . Kattie woulda been put away without her Momma . . . (*Iris nods.*) An' Joe need a place to bring his l'il Johnny Bull with the big ideas.

IRIS. I know that.

MARIE. (*Fiery.*) That's why the hell I'm here! (*Softer but still intense.*) There's the best goddamn bread in the world on that table . . . good coffee in the pot. It could be worse. Lotta folks ain't got that . . a place to be . . . somebody to love . . .

IRIS. I love . . . you . . . Marie. (*There's a moment.*)

MARIE. Ohh, honey . . . 'nother week or two, you'll be tellin'

73

Daddy off without no gun. (*Iris knows she's in danger of changing her mind and moves quickly to put her suitcase by the door.*)

IRIS. I don't think so.

MARIE. (*Following her.*) Maybe you do us all a big favor an' throw them damn rifles in the creek.

IRIS. (*She takes off the robe, revealing that she's dressed to go.*) No. I've got a bit more respect for guns now . . . certainly get things done, don't they?

MARIE. Don't talk like that.

IRIS. (*Putting on her coat.*) I'm ashamed to say this, but when I was holding that gun, I felt something I've never felt before. For once, I didn't feel like a cabbage: two grown men . . . backing away from me . . . frightened. I felt strong, really strong, Marie. But it wasn't a spiteful feeling. Matter of fact, I realized I had something in common with old Stephan. I knew he was feeling exactly the way I always feel . . . very small and far from home. And I felt ever so sorry for him. (*Passionately.*) But it's bloody-well coming to something, isn't it, when your strongest feelings happen with a gun in your hand? Give me a couple of years and I might get used to it. Well, *I don't want to get used to it.* (*Takes an envelope from her purse.*) Give this to Joe for me.

MARIE. Why you don't wait? Just till he's ready . . .

IRIS. Will he ever be ready?

MARIE. (*Hesitates, then goes to the hutch. She takes down an old tureen.*) For rainy day. I worked hard for rainy days. (*Takes out a roll of bills.*) I learn that from my Momma, God rest her . . . dime here . . . dollar there . . . come your time maybe you got enough to bury yourself. Here . . . (*Offers the money.*) But understand one thing, Iris . . . you go out that door, I ain't never gonna be able to speak your name again. I gotta stand by my son.

IRIS. I can't take your money.

MARIE. (*Loudly.*) *Take it!* (*Bangs the money on the table.*) You drag a baby from this house, you gonna need more'n a god-damn piggy bank! (*The baby begins to cry.*) Now look what you made me do. (*She hurries to the child and picks her up.*) Sssshhhh . . . Ssshhh . . .

IRIS. Give her your titty.

MARIE. No. We do it your way . . new way . . . (*Kisses the baby, gives her the pacifier.*) We teach her to leave the Mamma time for other things.

IRIS. I wish you could come with me, Marie.

MARIE. (*She attempts to hug her, but Marie resists by thrusting the baby firmly into it's mother's arms.*) Every time you say hello to sump'n new, you gotta say goodbye to sump'n old. Maybe you can do it. It's too late for me.

IRIS. In England, we say its never too late.

MARIE. (*Goes to door that leads upstairs, turns.*) Everybody's Old Country teach a lotta shit! (*She exits.*)

IRIS. (*To audience, after a pause.*) Oh, dear . . . forgot all about you. (*Glances tenderly at her baby.*) Not much left to tell, anyway. (*She goes to the back of the hutch and withdraws the sketch of Marie with her bread.*) I decided on New England because, as I told old Freda, it sounded like it was halfway between where I'd come from and where I'd been. (*Stands the sketch against a bowl on the table facing the audience.*) New Hampshire, actually . . . plenty of shoe factories I'd found out . . . and I supposed I'd be able to earn a living. (*Takes money with an air of regret and puts it in her pocket.*) I did take that money. Wouldn't have got far without it, would I? (*Goes to the door, opens it.*) Marie never wrote to me and I never sent a letter to her. Somebody might have found it. See, when I ended up on the "Dead and Deserted" list, next to old Pishta — as I knew I would — I didn't want anyone to say it was Marie's fault. Because it wasn't. (*Picks up suitcase.*) It wasn't anybody's fault. (*She leaves. Marie appears out of the shadows and calls to Katrine.*)

MARIE. Get outa Joe's bed, Kattie. Move! (*She examines the portrait of herself.*)

KATRINE. (*Entering.*) Iris said . . .

MARIE. Iris is gone.

KATRINE. Where?

MARIE. Just gone.

KATRINE. For good?

MARIE. Yeah.

KATRINE. (*Pause.*) Can I have my room back?

MARIE. We'll see. (*She tears up the sketch.*)

KATRINE. What you torn that for?

MARIE. (*Dropping it in the coal stove.*) I don't look that good.

(*She picks up her broom.*) How come you went to bed without sweepin' up this kitchen?

KATRINE. I was tired.

MARIE. What tired? Do I say tired? Get me the dustpan. Move! . . . you Hungarian elephant . . . before I smack you good. (*The lights fade quickly to black as the women go on with their work.*)

THE END

PROPERTY LIST

ACT I

Scene 1

Onstage

Cheap raincoat
Scarf
Outdoor clothing
Guns
Large wooden table
Hutch
Enamel pans (containing rising bread dough)
Damp towels
Straight-back chairs
Coal stove (enormous)
Wooden sink
Iron pump
Religious pictures
Family photographs (ancient)
Large, galvanized tubs (2)
Pan (of steaming Hungarian food)
Coffee pot
Accordian (old but beautiful)
Newspapers
Kerosene lamp
Telephone (brand-new, bright red)
Pan of rinse water
Broom
Screen
Aprons
Pail of water
Vodka
Glass
Plates
Pig's foot with hoof
Hunting rifle

Suitcases
Handbag (gold plastic)

Scene 2

Onstage

Large, high bed
Goosefeather ticks
Chest of drawers
Large enamel bucket (with lid)
Hand mirror
Lace panties
Bra
Mirror
Perfume
Mop
Pillows
Rugs

Offstage

Suitcase (packed)
Housedress (faded, long)
Babushka
High heel
Charm bracelet (cheap, in package) (both in suitcase)
Box

Scene 3

Onstage

Drawings of shoes
Towel
Car keys
Money (bills)
Laundry basket (heavy)
Babushka
Apron
Dustpan

Rifle (same as Scene 1)
Heavy coal bucket

Scene 4

Onstage

Crayons
Paper
Mixing bowl
High heel (from Scene 2)
Elaborate shoe designs
Towel
Coffee pot
Cups
Boots
Breakfast (eggs on plate)
Salt and pepper shakers
Bread
Suitcase
Pins

Offstage

Rifle (same as Scene 1)
Shirt (freshly ironed)
Socks (clean)
Red dress (very large, matronly, chiffon cocktail dress)
Envelopes (4) with birthday cards

ACT II

Scene 1

Onstage

Rocking chair
Knitting
Bread-making utensils
Coal
Bone

Babushka
Bread dough
Rifle (same as Act I)
Money (bills)
Feather duster
Hunting cap with earmuffs
Yellowed newspaper
Coffee pot
Cups

Offstage

Drawing (of wildflower)
Broom
Dusters

Scene 2

Onstage

Baseball cap
Pittsburgh Pirates pennant (taped to baby buggy)
Baby buggy
Cigars
Beer (1)
Accordian
Guns (2)
Handkerchief
Six-pack
Apron
Bread pans
Dough (covered by towel)

Offstage

Cigar
Heavy buckets of coal
Laundry basket
Ironing board

Scene 3

Onstage

Rolls
Clothing (two piles, neatly ironed)
Ironing board
Bread loaf

Offstage

Sketch pad

Scene 4

Onstage

Beer
Kerosene
Bucket
Rifle (same as Act I)
Bucket of water

Scene 5

Onstage

Suitcase
Long robe
Charm bracelet (from Act I)
Towel
Envelope
Teapot
Roll of bills
Pacifier
Sketch (Marie with bread)
Bowl
Broom

NEW
PLAYS

CARNAL KNOWLEDGE

THE LOMAN FAMILY PICNIC

THE MOONSHOT TAPE

A POSTER OF THE COSMOS

THE MODEL APARTMENT

AMATEURS

CARBONDALE DREAMS

SALLY BLANE, WORLD'S GREATEST
GIRL DETECTIVE

MOON OVER THE BREWERY

THE MEETING

THE STONEWATER RAPTURE

THE SHOW MUST GO ON

SEEING SOMEONE

IF WALLS COULD TALK

Write for information as to
availability
DRAMATISTS PLAY SERVICE, Inc.
440 Park Avenue South   New York, N.Y. 10016